Acknowledgments for this Book

I wish to thank Dr. Harold Carter for his assistance in the editing of this book and the many hours he spent with me during the creation of the book. Hal's support and encouragement are appreciated very much.

I wish to thank Caroline Carter (my sister) and Harry and Forest Conn (my parents) for their support and encouragement. They are always there when I need them.

Finally, thanks to Elizabeth Feinler and the individuals at the Network Information Center, and Frank Wancho and the individuals at White Sands Missile Range, and other individuals using SIMTEL20 who always seem to find time to answer my questions.

Ada Software Repository Acknowledgments

Many individuals have contributed to the Ada Software Repository (ASR) in a variety of ways, ranging from writing and contributing software to providing political support to expending effort to evaluate, correlate, and distribute the submissions to the ASR. Their efforts are greatly appreciated.

Thanks to Frank Wancho at White Sands for his political support, technical assistance, and general guidance and direction.

Thanks to Colonel William Whitaker and Lt Colonel Terry Courtwright of WIS JPMO for their political support and for making the submission of the WIS Tools possible.

Thanks to Mark Greinke, Tana Reagan, Mike McClimens, Robert Hutchinson, and Dr. Michael Gardner of MITRE for their efforts in evaluating, correlating, and submitting the WIS Tools to the ASR. Thanks also to them for their individual and corporate contributions.

Several people at WIS JPMO should also be recognized and thanked for their support: Lt Colonel Frank Falgiano, Captain Jacques Choiniere, and Captain James Wedertz.

Two people in particular should be thanked for their efforts in supporting the tape distribution at White Sands: Dave Tapiá, who creates the tapes between doing his other duties, and Debbie Narvaez, who packs and mails the tapes (largely on her own time).

Thanks to Frank Gaudè at Echelon for his support in answering users' questions, publishing the ASR Newsletter, and publishing the Master Index.

Last, but by no means least, thanks to all of those individuals, specifically named in the Prologue files in the ASR, who unselfishly contributed their software to the ASR. Without these people and their contributions, the spirit of the free sharing of software promoted by the ASR could not be achieved.

Richard Conn

THE ADA SOFTWARE REPOSITORY AND THE DEFENSE DATA NETWORK

A Resource Handbook

RICHARD CONNN

NEW YORK ZOETROPE

THE ADA SOFTWARE REPOSITORY AND THE DEFENSE DATA NETWORK
A Resource Handbook

Library of Congress Cataloging in Publication Number: 86-43222

ISBN 0-918432-78-2

New York Zoetrope
838 Broadway
New York, NY 10003

The Ada Software Repository and DDN Resource Handbook was set in H-P Times Roman. The book was printed and bound by Crane Duplicating Services, at their West Barnstaple, MA plant.

Printed in the United States of America
First Printing: December, 1986
5 4 3 2 1

Contents

Figures

Chapter 1

Introduction

Computer networking is rapidly changing our lives, impacting the way we interact with each other, the speed and efficiency with which we exchange information, and the way we conduct our everyday business. The computer networks are promoting a free exchange of information in a manner and on an order of magnitude unlike anything society has experienced, and knowledge of these networks and their effective use is becoming essential to the scientist in general and the computer professional in particular. The community of computer professionals has been divided into two classes—those with access to the major networks and those without—and access to the major networks is becoming such a necessity that the number of people without such access is growing smaller and smaller each day.

1.1 The Defense Data Network, the Internet

The largest of such networks is the Defense Data Network (DDN) of the United States Department of Defense (DoD), but the DDN is not just a computer network. The DDN, also known as the Internet, is a network of over 400 computer networks. Each computer on these networks uses the same Transmission Control Protocol/Internet Protocol (TCP/IP), shares a common name and address space (which facilitates the transfer of electronic mail and files), and can communicate with any other computer on any other network of the Internet.

The Internet exists for several reasons:

1. It provides a common, reliable, rugged, and secure communications path between organizations within the DoD, including the

White House, the Pentagon, and all major DoD commands.

2. It facilitates the sharing of resources between organizations on the Internet (which include many universities, national research laboratories, and commercial research centers).

3. It facilitates communication between people at the organizations on the Internet.

4. It provides a testbed for further developments in computer networking.

The operation of the Internet is coordinated by the DDN Network Information Center (NIC) at SRI International in Menlo Park, California, and the DDN Network Operations Center (NOC) at Bolt, Beranek, and Newman (BBN) in Cambridge, Massachusetts. The two main networks comprising the Internet, namely the ARPANET (sponsored by the Defense Advanced Research Projects Agency for computer network research) and the MILNET (sponsored by the DoD for use by military organizations), are funded by government grants and DoD directives. Many of the other networks, such as MINET (the military intelligence network) and BRLNET (the network at the Ballistic Research Lab at Aberdeen Proving Ground), are also funded by DoD directives, while others, such as CMU-NET (at Carnegie-Mellon University) and FORDNET (for Ford Corporation), are funded by local organizations. Still other networks, particularly CSNET (the Computer Science Network, which is partly in the Internet and partly out of the Internet), are funded by both the DoD and private organizations.

The Internet was designed for growth, and it is constantly evolving—new networks and *host computers* are added almost daily. (A host computer supports one or more users and is directly connected to a network of the Internet). There are vast resources in constant use on the Internet, such as the huge software repositories at the SIMTEL20 and CU20B nodes, the large base of information on the Internet at SRI-NIC, and over 100 electronic mailing lists on subjects ranging from microcomputer software to the

US space program. These resources, too, are changing, and their rate of growth is virtually exponential.

1.2 This Book

This book introduces its readers to the operation and resources of the Internet, with particular emphasis on the Ada Software Repository on SIMTEL20. The book provides current answers, and pointers to future answers, to such questions as: What facilities are available on the Internet? How can the user access them? How can the user keep up with them and adapt as they change? This book is not comprehensive; I don't think that any one person or organization really knows the entire scope of resources provided by the Internet. However, this book does present answers to many fundamental questions and, perhaps more importantly, it provides pointers to the ways in which you'll be able to use the available resources in order to find the answers to questions that haven't yet been asked.

This book is divided into four main sections: an introduction to the Defense Data Network and its use; an introduction to the SIMTEL20 host computer on the MILNET and its software repositories; the Ada Software Repository on SIMTEL20; and other resources on the Defense Data Network.

The first section, on the Defense Data Network as a whole, introduces the reader to the DDN by way of its history and capabilities. This section is a guide to users and provides an introductory discussion of the fundamental tools, such as electronic mail; Telnet (a remote login capability); FTP (the File Transfer Protocol used for transferring files between DDN host computers); and the microcomputer communications protocols used for transferring files between DDN host computers and a user's personal computer.

The second section presents further detail on these and other facilities available on the SIMTEL20 host computer. The section begins with a history and overview of SIMTEL20 and its software repositories. Since these repositories are among the resources that you'll probably want to access, the section next presents a user's view of SIMTEL20 and its operating system, TOPS-20. There's a discussion of the electronic mailing lists employed in support of users of the software repositories; finally, and perhaps most importantly, you'll find detailed instructions on how to obtain software from the repositories by using FTP, the Archive Server, and the tape distribution.

Because the DoD, the universities, and industry have all shown enormous interest in the Ada Software Repository and the Ada programming language, the third section describes, in considerable detail, the current structure, content and operation of the Ada Software Repository (ASR). The ASR is somewhat different from the other repositories on SIMTEL20. Like the other repositories, ASR provides an electronic mailing list in support of users of the ASR. However, unlike the other repositories, ASR also provides detailed hardcopy documentation in the form of *The Master Index to the Ada Software Repository*; hardcopy and machine-readable newsletters; a machine-readable data base; and support software for accessing this data base.

The fourth section describes other resources of the Defense Data Network. Four main resources are covered here: the Network Information Center and its data bases; Columbia University's CU20B host computer and its Kermit distributions; the ADA20 host computer and its wealth of Ada-related information; and many of the popular electronic mailing lists.

Finally, the appendices provide pointers to more information. These pointers are stepping stones by means of which the reader can go beyond the bounds of this book and acquire access to the DDN resources which support his specific needs.

This book is intended to be a living document, changing and growing with the needs of its readers. Its basic information, its current layout and presentations, and its pointers are just a starting point. For this reason, each section begins with a section outline which is followed by a blank page on which the user can make his own notes. As it evolves, with feedback from readers, this book should serve as a handy reference for the use of the Internet. Your comments will be welcome. Feel free to contact the author via ADA-SW-REQUEST@SIMTEL20.ARPA which is soon to be:

ADA-SW-REQUEST@SIMTEL20.MIL. Enjoy!

Richard Conn

October 20, 1986

SECTION I: THE DEFENSE DATA NETWORK

– Outline –

Chapter 2

History and Overview of the Defense Data Network

In April 1982, the United States Department of Defense (DoD) directed that the Defense Data Network (DDN) be implemented as the world-wide DoD data communications network. The Office of the Secretary of Defense directed that:

"All DoD ADP [Automatic Data Processing] systems and data networks requiring data communications services will be provided long-haul and area communications, interconnectivity, and the capability for interoperability by the DDN. Existing systems, systems being expanded and upgraded, and new ADP systems or data networks will become DDN subscribers."

The Defense Communications Agency (DCA) now has operational responsibility and control of the Defense Data Network.

2.1 Packet Switching Networks

In August 1964, Paul Baran of the Rand Corporation prepared an eleven-volume analysis titled *On Distributed Communications* as a deliverable item of an Air Force contract. This study proposed a distributed packet switching system to provide for all military communications, data, and voice. The Air Force, however, took no further action and the report was largely ignored until Donald Davies, of the National Physical Laboratory in England, independently rediscovered packet switching. Davies' proposed network design was circulated through the U.K. in late 1965 and 1966; it was only after this distribution that Davies discovered Baran's earlier report.

Lawrence Roberts joined the DoD's Advanced Research Projects Agency (ARPA) in January 1967, assuming the management of the computer research programs sponsored by ARPA at many leading universities and research laboratories in the United States. During 1967, the ARPANET was conceived as a means to link computers at those sites. The ARPANET plan was published in June 1967, and a request for proposal (RFP) was awarded to Bolt Beranek and Newman, Inc. (BBN) of Cambridge, Massachusetts, in January 1969. The BBN team, consisting of Frank Heart, Robert Kahn, Severo Ornstein, William Crowther, and David Walden, successfully designed, installed, and brought four nodes of the network into operation by December 1969. The ARPANET was born, and it has grown rapidly and continuously:

April 1971	23 host computers
June 1974	62 host computers
March 1977	111 host computers
Today	Over 400 computer networks

Robert Kahn of BBN organized the first public demonstration of packet switching at the First International Conference on Computer Communications (ICCC) at Washington, DC, in October 1972. He installed an ARPANET node at the conference hotel, allowing 40 terminals at the hotel to access many computers all over the United States. This demonstration convinced many important people that packet switching worked, and thereby established ARPANET as the father of all packet switching networks. By 1974, the number of operational users of the ARPANET had grown so large that the Defense Communications Agency (DCA) assumed operational responsibility.

In 1974, the DoD began planning for a packet-switching network to connect the computers and terminals in the DoD community. This network was to provide features, particularly in the area of communications security, required by the DoD but not offered by the ARPANET or any other commercial packet-switching networks. The Defense Communications Agency (DCA) awarded a contract to Western Union in 1976 to develop such a network, called AUTODIN II (AUTODIN I was a message-switching, as opposed to packet-switching, network that Western Union leased to the government beginning in the early 1960's). AUTODIN II reached Initial Operational Capability in July 1981, but between 1976 and 1981 the United States government placed increasing emphasis on reducing the cost of communications and improving the ability of computer networks to survive a major catastrophe. In April 1982, therefore, as the result of a study done by DCA and the Defense Science Board, the DoD terminated the AUTODIN II project and directed that the Defense Data Network, based upon the existing ARPANET and its technology, be implemented.

2.2 What is Packet Switching?

Packet switching is a method of transmitting data through a communications network. In a packet-switching computer network, message processors to which computers and terminals are attached divide messages into small packets, then route and process each packet as though it were a separate and independent message. Each switching node (which includes a message processor) in a packet-switching network receives a packet, checks for and corrects errors in the packet, and then either forwards the packet to another node or collects all of the packets of a message and delivers the entire message to a local addressee (which is usually a host computer that is physically connected to the node).

As a packet-switching network, the Defense Data Network routes packets adaptively rather than along predetermined paths. The *adaptive routing* feature allows switching nodes to route packets around portions of the DDN that are congested or have been damaged by a line failure or a hardware failure. Further, all data errors detected during transmission result in the automatic retransmission of the erroneous packet. The reliability of communications is very important on the DDN, and the expected undetected error rate is 4.2E-18 or less. This means that if a user were to send a full packet (over 8000 bits) every second, without interruption, a bit error would slip through the DDN undetected only once every million years.

Chapter 3

DDN Capabilities and Tools

Users of the Defense Data Network employ three basic software tools in their interaction with the computers and other users of the network. These tools are:

1. Electronic mail, for sending electronic mail messages to other users and to special programs (such as the Archive Server on SIMTEL20) on various DDN host computers;
2. The File Transfer Protocol (FTP), for efficiently transferring text and binary files between two host computers on the DDN; and
3. TELNET, for linking through one DDN host computer to another as an interactive user.

The vast majority of DDN users employ only electronic mail and have not used FTP or TELNET. Those DDN users who want easy access to the repositories on SIMTEL20 should learn how to use FTP to accomplish this access. TELNET is a convenience for DDN users who frequently use more than one host computer, particularly if they transfer files between their accounts on different host computers.

3.1 Electronic Mail

Electronic mail on the DDN ties you into a fantastic wealth of information and resources. You can use electronic mail on a personal level (for person-to-person communications), on a public level (for person-to-group communications), and on a tool level (for person-to-program communications).

Two colleagues can communicate and work together via electronic mail, regardless of the physical distance separating them. You can send or receive small files (usually less than 50K bytes) via electronic mail; such files may contain programs, chapters of books that are being developed, technical papers and their abstracts, and many other items. As more people tie into the networks, it is becoming more and more common to submit abstracts and papers to conferences, and to plan meetings and other events, via electronic mail. Electronic mail provides the convenience of a timely communications medium that you can use when you're ready to sit down and work on a particular project–whereas the US mail is very slow, and telephone calls can often be an annoying distraction from urgent work.

There are many electronic mailing lists through which users who share similar interests communicate with each other. Often, if you send an electronic mail message to a special address, the programs at that address can duplicate the message, sending a copy to each of the mailing list subscribers. Electronic mailing lists can also use digests; in this mode of operation, messages for distribution all go to the person acting as the moderator or coordinator of the list. That person edits or augments the messages in some way, and then collects them into a single larger digest message that he sends to the list subscribers periodically.

On the tool level, certain programs running on the DDN receive commands from electronic mail messages, process those commands, and send electronic mail back to the sender of the message. The Archive Server on SIMTEL20, for instance, is a tool to which users send electronic mail messages that contain commands like "SEND DIR" to send a directory display back to the user or "SEND FILE" to send a specific file back to the user. The MOSIS project at USC employs a tool to which users send electronic mail messages that contain integrated circuit (IC) designs in a specified format; upon receiving such messages, the tool processes them (causing the ICs to be fabricated), and provides workers at USC with mailing instructions for the newly created ICs.

Figures 3-1, 3-2, and 3-3 show a sample electronic mail session. Text entered by the user is in *italics*.

```
@mm
SIMTEL20.ARPA.#Internet MM-20 6.1(1112)
 Last read: 22-Oct-86 00:19:15, 48 messages, 30 pages
 13 messages unseen
Mail>headers 36:*
 U   36) 19-Oct Steve Minneman  Re: Copyrights (2076 chars)
 U   37) 19-Oct "Willie Smith,  S-100 definition (1026 chars)
 U   38) 19-Oct liber%darth.uuc Device Driver (1754 chars)
 U   39) 20-Oct Tony Li         ZCPR on a DEC VT180 (799 chars)
 U   40) 20-Oct Keith Petersen  FTP file transfers from
             SIMTEL20  (1258 chars)
 U   41) 20-Oct LIN@mit-xx.ARPA SCAN12 (538 chars)
 U   42) 20-Oct Keith Petersen  Quick reference list of
             SIMTEL20  (2668 chars)
 U   43) 20-Oct Ted Medin       Re: Query: Z-system availability
             (386 chars)
 U   44) 20-Oct HOSTMASTER@SRI- Re: IMP/Host Numbering
             Question (1301 chars)
 U   45) 20-Oct prindle@nadc.AR .LLB vs .LBR ??? (780 chars)
 U   46) 21-Oct PSY%SEUMDC51.BI (This is optional)
             (389 chars)
 U   47) 21-Oct WANCHO@SIMTEL20 .LLB vs .LBR ???
             (777 chars)
 U   48) 21-Oct UZ32112%BLIULG1 NOTE from UZ32112
             (1086 chars)
```

Figure 3–1. *Electronic Mail - Entering MM and Displaying Headers*

```
Mail>type 41
 Message 41 (538 characters):
Return-Path: <info-cpm-request@AMSAA.ARPA>
Received: from AMSAA by SIMTEL20.ARPA with TCP; Mon
        20 Oct 86 08:49:03-MDT
Received: from mit-xx.arpa by AMSAA.ARPA id a003994; 18
        Oct 86 15:47 EDT
Date: Sat, 18 Oct 1986  15:51 EDT
Message-ID: <LIN.12247846728.BABYL@XX.LCS.MIT.EDU>
From: LIN@mit-xx.ARPA
To:  info-cpm@AMSAA.ARPA
Subject: SCAN12
Resent-Date:  Mon, 20 Oct 86 8:04:14 EDT
Resent-From:  info-cpm@AMSAA.ARPA
Resent-To:    info-cpm-relay@mit-xx.ARPA

Does anyone have the source code to SCAN 1.2 anywhere?

Thanks.
```

Figure 3–2. Electronic Mail - Typing a Message

```
Mail>send
To: newuser@simtel20.arpa
cc:
Subject: Welcome to the ASR
Message (End with ESCAPE or CTRL/Z.
 Use CTRL/B to insert a file, CTRL/E to enter editor,
        CTRL/K to redisplay
 message, CTRL/L to clear screen and redisplay, CTRL/N
        to abort.):
Welcome to the Ada Software Repository. You are now on the
        electronic
mailing list ADA-SW. An introductory message will be
        forthcoming.

     Rick Conn
^Z
Send>send
 newuser@SIMTEL20.ARPA.#Internet -- queued
Mail>exit
```

Figure 3–3. Electronic Mail - Sending a Message

3.2

File Transfer Protocol

The File Transfer Protocol (FTP) tools let you transfer files from one DDN host computer to another. You start the process by running the FTP program on your local host computer, telling the program that you wish to connect with another DDN host computer. FTP makes the connection with this remote host computer, causing a program known as an FTP Server to run there (see Figure 3-4). You then type a login command to your local FTP program, which in turn communicates with the remote FTP Server to log you into the remote computer. Once logged in, you can issue a variety of commands (the commands available to you depend on the nature of the FTP program and the FTP Server). Most systems support the following commands:

1. GET (sometimes called RECEIVE) - transfers one or more files from the remote computer to the local computer.
2. PUT (sometimes called SEND) - transfers one or more files from the local computer to the remote computer.
3. DIR - sends a directory display from the remote computer to the local computer.
4. CD (sometimes called CWD) - moves the user to another default directory on the remote host computer.
5. QUIT (sometimes called EXIT) - terminates the communication shutting down both the FTP Server program on the remote computer and the FTP program on the local computer.

```
 ---------------      --------------      --------
| Remote Host |      | Local Host  |     |        |
|  Computer   |______|  Computer   |_____|  User  |
| Runs FTP    |      | Runs FTP    |     |        |
|  Server     |      |             |     |        |
 ---------------      --------------      --------
```

Figure 3–4. Running FTP

Figure 3-5 shows a sample FTP session. Text typed by the user is in *italics.*

@*ftp remote-host*
< remote-host TCP FTP Service (Version 3.00) at Tue Oct 21
        23:15-PST
Setting default transfer type to text.
FTP>*login remoteid*
Password:
< User logged in, default directory DRB2:[REMOTEID]
FTP>*get motd.txt*
motd.txt (to local file) *demo.txt*
motd.txt => <RCONN>DEMO.TXT.1;P777700 !! [OK]
FTP>*quit*

Figure 3–5. A Sample FTP Session

3.3

TELNET

The TELNET tool allows you to login as an interactive user on a remote host computer via your local host computer. To be exact, you can invoke and run TELNET on one computer after another on the DDN, extending the chain until you are are interacting with all of them at the same time. For example, you might employ FTP to send a file to a remote computer, then use TELNET to log into that remote computer, check your file, and finally drop back to your local host computer.

Consult your local systems people for more details on the use of your local TELNET implementation. Figure 3-6 shows a sample TELNET session. Text typed by the user is in *italics*.

@*telnet remote-host*
Trying... Open
Username: *remoteid*
Password:
Welcome to VAX/VMS version V4.4
Last interactive login on Wednesday, 8-OCT-1986 09:10
Last non-interactive login on Thursday, 27-FEB-1986 19:17

^^ NOTICE^^
CHANGE ORACLE REFERENCES FROM DJA2: TO DRB3:

DBA4: USERS HAVE BEEN RELOCATED TO DRB2:
CHANGE LOGICAL
REFERENCES FROM DBA4: TO DRB2: IN YOUR
LOGIN/DEFINITION FILES

$ *<commands are now issued interactively with remote host computer>*

$ *logout*
REMOTEID logged out at 21-OCT-1986 23:14:52.08

Connection closed by foreign host

Figure 3–6. A Sample TELNET Session

Chapter 4

Electronic Mail

4.1

Electronic Mail on the DDN

Electronic mail is one of the most useful services provided by the Defense Data Network. Using electronic mail, you can send messages to another DDN user, to a group of DDN users, or to a special software system that receives its commands via electronic mail.

4.2

Addresses

In order to send an electronic message, you must know the correct address of the recipient. These addresses (as expressed from the DDN side) always take the form:

designator@DDN_host

where *designator* identifies the recipient in some way, @ is a delimiter, and *DDN_HOST* identifies the DDN host computer through which the recipient receives his electronic mail. In some cases, the recipient has an account on the indicated host computer; in other cases, the host computer acts as a *gateway*, forwarding the electronic mail messages to another computer or computer network. Case is not usually significant; that is, a host sees jsmith as being identical to JSMITH and JSmith. The notable exception to this rule is the message addressed to a MULTICS system (MULTICS, an operating system that runs on Honeywell mainframes, is case-sensitive). For example,

1. JSMITH@ADA20.ISI.EDU is the address of an individual who has an account on the indicated DDN host computer, ADA20.ISI.EDU.

2.
CHAN%SYSTEMX@RELAY.CS.NET is the address of an individual identified as CHAN who has an account on SYSTEMX. SYSTEMX is reached through the DDN host computer RELAY.CS.NET (this is the CSNET relay computer, a gateway between CSNET and the DDN).

3.
"ihnp4!floyd!bonnie!clyde!jblow"@SEISMO.CSS.GOV is the address of an individual on USENET. USENET, a network of UNIX systems, is accessed through several DDN host computers; in this case, SEISMO.CSS.GOV is the DDN host computer chosen to act as the gateway between USENET and the DDN. The user's address is a path, indicating to the mailer how to route the message through the USENET. The message is sent by SEISMO.CSS.GOV to ihnp4, then floyd, then bonnie, then clyde, and finally to user jblow on clyde. In order to avoid conflicts and other confusion on the DDN side of this address, the routing path recognized by USENET is quoted; quoting a designator instructs the DDN to pass the designator to the DDN host without any interpretation.

4.
"22337J7%XSYSTEM.BITNET"@WISCVM.WISC.EDU is an address of a user on BITNET, and the electronic mail message is gatewayed through the DDN host WISCVM.WISC.EDU. Again, the designator is quoted so that the DDN will not do any interpretation; the quote marks are not always necessary, but you'll probably never lose if you consistently put them in.

Some of the more common forms of address from the DDN to other networks are shown in Figure 4-1.

To	*Address*
BITNET	user%host.BITNET@WISCVM.WISC.EDU
CSNET	user%host.CSNET@RELAY.CS.NET
CSNET	user%host@RELAY.CS.NET
DDN	user@DDN_host
Easynet (DEC)	user%host.DEC@DECWRL.DEC.COM
MAILNET	user%host.MAILNET@MIT-MULTICS.ARPA
USENET/UUCP	host1!host2!...!user@ddn_gateway
UUCP	user%host.UUCP@ddn_gateway
VNET (IBM)	user%host@IBM.COM

Figure 4-1. Common DDN Message Address Forms

To simplify the addressing problem, most electronic mail programs on DDN hosts provide an ANSWER or REPLY command. The mail program figures out what the return address should be and fills this address in for the user.

4.3

Newsgroup Correspondence Archives

Copies of correspondence for several newsgroups are kept on SIMTEL20 in directories with names of the form PS:<ARCHIVES.KEYWORD>, where "KEYWORD" has been chosen to indicate the associated newsgroup. For instance, PS:<ARCHIVES.CPM> is the SIMTEL20 directory name for the INFO-CPM newsgroup (electronic mailing list). Many correspondence archives are currently available (see Figure 4-2).

newsgroup	*mail archive filename*
ADA-SW	PS:<ARCHIVES.ADA-SW>
AMETHYST-USERS	PS:<ARCHIVES.AMETHYST>
INFO-68K	PS:<ARCHIVES.68K>
INFO-APPLE	PS:<ARCHIVES.APPLE>
INFO-CPM	PS:<ARCHIVES.CPM>
INFO-FORTH	PS:<ARCHIVES.FORTH>
INFO-HAMS	PS:<ARCHIVES.HAMS>
INFO-MICRO	PS:<ARCHIVES.MICRO>
INFO-MODEM7	PS:<ARCHIVES.MODEM7>
INFO-MODEMXX	PS:<ARCHIVES.MODEMXX>
INFO-MODULA-2	PS:<ARCHIVES.MODULA-2>
NORTHSTAR-USERS	PS:<ARCHIVES.NORTHSTAR>
INFO-PASCAL	PS:<ARCHIVES.PASCAL>
UNIX-SW	PS:<ARCHIVES.UNIX-SW>
INFO-XENIX310	PS:<ARCHIVES.XENIX310>

Figure 4–2. Electronic Mail Archives

Descriptions of these and other newsgroups can be obtained via FTP with anonymous login (see the section on FTP) from the Network Information Center's host SRI-NIC.ARPA. Use FTP to get the file PS:<NETINFO>INTEREST-GROUPS.TXT (an ASCII file).

File names for SIMTEL20 newsgroup correspondence archives have two forms. For example, PS:<ARCHIVES.CPM>CPM.ARCHIV.ymmdd is a group of files containing INFO-CPM correspondence going back several years. The characters "ymmdd" in a file name are digits that give the year, month and day of the last message in that file. You'll find current correspondence in the file PS:<ARCHIVES.CPM>CPM-ARCHIV.TXT, which is constantly changing. Although INFO-CPM has been used as an example here, the other newsgroup files use the same naming scheme. For a complete list of available files, connect to SIMTEL20 via FTP and give the command (in FTP):

dir ps:<archives>

You will receive a list of names of the form:

KEYWORD.DIRECTORY.n

where "n" is one or more digits. For example, the INFO-CPM listing currently appears as "CPM.DIRECTORY.1". Then, to get a list of files in a particular archive, give the command (in FTP):

dir ps:<archives.keyword>

where "keyword" (for example, "CPM") is chosen from the newsgroup list above. At present, all of these files are stored in ASCII format.

4.4 SAM

SAM is a communications and mail management software package that extends the DDN electronic mail facility to a personal computer that is employed by the user to communicate with the DDN through a TAC. Sold by the DDN Network Information Center (NIC), SAM runs on an IBM PC (or compatible) with two floppy-disk drives and at least 256K bytes of RAM (you'll need 320K bytes if you want to use Kermit with SAM). SAM is not copy-protected and currently supports the following host-computer-based electronic mail programs: VMS mail, UNIX mail, InfoMail, and MM. SAM has been tested by DARPA (the Defense Advanced Research Projects Agency), NSF (the National Science Foundation), and the DDN PMO (the Defense Data Network Project Management Office).

SAM lets you:

1. Connect to a DDN host computer through a TAC;
2. Retrieve any messages sent to the user from the host computer onto the user's PC;
3. Read and compose electronic mail on your PC; and
4. Transmit electronic mail messages from your PC through a TAC to the DDN host computer and automatically mail those messages to the addresses.

SAM saves you connect time and reduces the frustrations of working on a heavily-loaded DDN host computer. SAM is both easy for beginners to use and adaptable so that you can make it more convenient as you become more experienced. Using SAM, you can log into a TAC, make host connections, and reach across the DDN to use services like WHOIS and TACNEWS.

For more information on SAM (including current prices and how to order it), contact the NIC at 800-235-3155 or 415-859-3695. You can get answers to your questions by sending electronic mail to SAM@SRI-NIC.ARPA. Both individual purchases and site license arrangements can be made, and training is available.

Chapter 5

Domain Names on the DDN

Host computers on the Defense Data Network were, in the past, given simple names, such as SIMTEL20 or ADA20 that were known to all hosts on the DDN. Names started with a letter, ended with a letter or digit, and contained only letters, digits, or a hyphen in the body of the name. Case was not significant. These simple names are still recognized and used by the standard DDN tools: electronic mail, the File Transfer Protocol (FTP), and TELNET. For example:

FTP SIMTEL20
 – runs FTP, connecting to SIMTEL20
TELNET SIMTEL20
 – runs TELNET, connecting to SIMTEL20
ADA-SW@SIMTEL20
 – the electronic mail address for the ADA-SW email list based on SIMTEL20

Because of the growth of the Internet, structured names (or *domain style names*) have been introduced. Each component of a structured name is unique only within the scope of the superior component name; thus, given top-level component names like ARPA and MIL (for the ARPANET and MILNET parts of the DDN), it is possible for MYHOST.ARPA (a computer on the ARPANET) and MYHOST.MIL (a different computer on the MILNET) to coexist on the DDN, whereas formerly only one computer could be named MYHOST.

Each element of a structured name is a character string that follows the same constraints as did the older simple names (as presented in the previous paragraph). The components are ordered from right to left and separated by periods, with the upper-level components on the far right. Examples of such names are SIMTEL20.ARPA, USC-ISIF.ISI.EDU, SEISMO.CSS.GOV, and ADA20.ISI.EDU. In these examples, the top-level domains are ARPA (for ARPANET), EDU (for Educational institutions), and GOV (for Government facility). In addition, ADA20 and USC-ISIF are a part of the ISI component under the top-level EDU component.

The introduction of these structured names to the DDN has been limited so far; as an intermediate measure, every name on the DDN has been converted to the original simple name with a top-level component of ARPA (such as SIMTEL20.ARPA, where the original simple name was SIMTEL20). This is a temporary situation, however, and according to present plans the ARPA domain will eventually cease to exist. All host computers will eventually change their names as the domain style names come into full use, but the conversion process will take many years to complete.

5.1 Current Top-Level Domains

As of 26 September, 1986, fifteen top-level domains have been registered with the DDN Network Information Center. These domains are named in Figure 5-1.

ARPA	AU	COM	EDU	FR
GOV	IL	JP	MIL	NET
NL	ORG	SE	UK	US

Figure 5–1. Top-Level Domains of the DDN

5.2 Current Second-Level Domains

As of 26 September, 1986, over 120 second-level domains have been registered with the DDN Network Information Center. These domains are named in Figures 5-2, 5-3, and 5-4.

COM (Commercial) Top-Level Domain:

ADELIE.COM	ATT.COM	BBN.COM
BELL-ATL.COM	BELLCORE.COM	BOEING.COM
BUCK.COM	CCA.COM	DEC.COM
FMC.COM	GE.COM	GMR.COM
GREBYN.COM	HP.COM	IBM.COM
INTEL.COM	ISC.COM	ITCORP.COM
MCC.COM	NBI.COM	NEXT.COM
NORTHROP.COM	NSC.COM	OLIVETTI.COM
PROTEON.COM	PYR.COM	RCA.COM
SRI.COM	STARGATE.COM	SUN.COM
SYMBOLICS.COM	TEK.COM	THINK.COM
TI.COM	TMC.COM	UB.COM
VSE.COM	XEROX.COM	

Figure 5–2. 8A: DDN Domain Names - Commercial

EDU (Educational) Top-Level Domain:

ARIZONA.EDU	BERKELEY.EDU	BGSU.EDU
BROWN.EDU	BU.EDU	BUFFALO.EDU
CALTECH.EDU	CARLETON.EDU	CMU.EDU
COLGATE.EDU	COLORADO.EDU	COLUMBIA.EDU
CORNELL.EDU	DARTMOUTH.EDU	DEPAUL.EDU
DU.EDU	DUKE.EDU	EMORY.EDU
GATECH.EDU	HARVARD.EDU	INDIANA.EDU
ISI.EDU	LEHIGH.EDU	MICH-STATE.EDU
MIT.EDU	MOSIS.EDU	NORTHEASTERN.EDU
OGC.EDU	OKSTATE.EDU	PITTSBURGH.EDU
PSU.EDU	PURDUE.EDU	RIACS.EDU
RICE.EDU	RPI.EDU	RUTGERS.EDU
SDSU.EDU	SJU.EDU	STANFORD.EDU
SUNYSB.EDU	SYR.EDU	TMC.EDU
TORONTO.EDU	UAB.EDU	UCDAVIS.EDU
UCHICAGO.EDU	UCI.EDU	UCLA.EDU
UCSD.EDU	UCSF.EDU	UDEL.EDU
UFL.EDU	UIOWA.EDU	UIUC.EDU
UKANS.EDU	UMASS.EDU	UMB.EDU
UMD.EDU	UMICH.EDU	UNC.EDU
UNLV.EDU	UNM.EDU	UOREGON.EDU
UPENN.EDU	USC.EDU	USL.EDU
UTA.EDU	UTEXAS.EDU	UWP.EDU
VILLANOVA.EDU	VIRGINIA.EDU	VT.EDU
WANGINST.EDU	WASHINGTON.EDU	WATERLOO.EDU
WELLESLEY.EDU	WFU.EDU	WISC.EDU
WKU.EDU	WRIGHT.EDU	

Figure 5–3. 8B: DDN Domain Names - Educational

GOV (Special Government Organizations) Top-Level Domain:

CSS.GOV DSPO.GOV NASA.GOV

MIL (MILNET) Top-Level Domain:

BRL.MIL DARPA.MIL NOSC.MIL

NET (Other Networks) Top-Level Domain:

CS.NET

ORG (Special Organizations) Top-Level Domain:

CSC.ORG MCNC.ORG MITRE.ORG SRC.ORG SUPER.ORG

UK (United Kingdom) Top-Level Domain:

AC.UK

Figure 5-4. 8C: DDN Domain Names - Government and Other

5.3 NIC Information

Most DDN host computers have a facility called *WHOIS*, which allows users to directly query the data base at the Network Information Center (NIC). This is particularly useful in finding out information about the domains. In order to find the contacts for a domain, give the command:

WHOIS domain_name

such as:

WHOIS MIT.EDU

Chapter 6

TACs and TAC Commands

Many users of the Defense Data Network access the network through a computer called a Terminal Access Controller (TAC). A TAC is a communications switch that connects groups of users to the Defense Data Network, and usually works in conjunction with two Interface Message Processors (IMP), one at the host end of the line and the other at the TAC end. Figure 6-1 shows this connection in diagram form. The TAC provides a transparent connection to a host computer, allowing you to communicate with the DDN host computer as if you were directly connected to it. In most cases, every character you type on your keyboard passes through the TAC to the Interface Message Processor (IMP), which assembles your characters into packets and sends these packets to the remote host computer via the DDN. The host's IMP disassembles the packets it receives and passes the individual characters to the host computer, which appends them to the appropriate memory buffer until the message is complete. Likewise, characters sent by the remote host computer are assembled by the host's IMP into packets for transmission over the line. The TAC's IMP extracts the characters from the packets and, using the packet address, tells the TAC how to route them to the appropriate user.

The user's equipment may be either a simple computer terminal or a personal computer. If you're using terminal, the host computer and the TAC provide all the software needed. If you're using a personal computer, you'll need to run one of the many telecommunications programs that are available for transferring files through the network between the personal computer and the remote host computer.

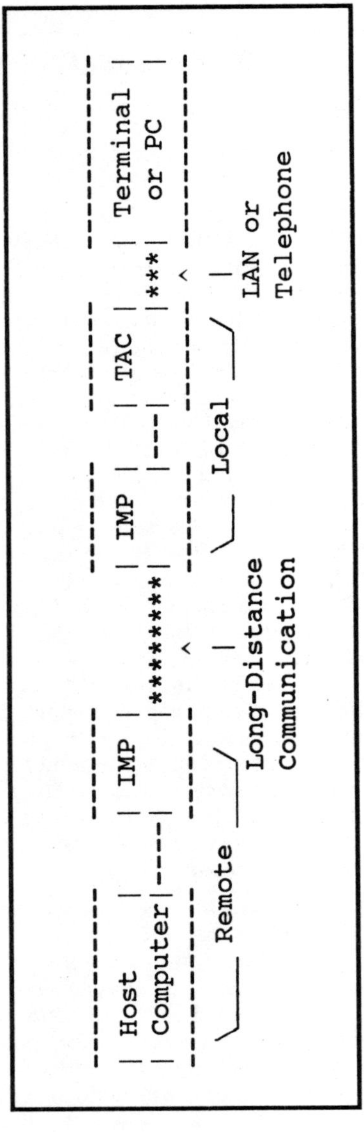

Figure 6–1. DDN Connectivity

A DDN TAC supports the DoD standard host-to-host computer communications protocol, called the Transmission Control Protocol/Internet Protocol (TCP/IP), as the backbone of the DDN communications capability. Many other protocols are employed on top of TCP/IP, such as the Simple Mail Transfer Protocol (SMTP) for the transfer of mail between host computers, the File Transfer Protocol (FTP) for the transfer of files between host computers, and Kermit and XMODEM for the transfer of files between a host computer and a personal computer that is connected to the host computer via a TAC. For more information, see the RFCs (Requests for Comments) referenced in the Further Reading appendix.

A second scenario also exists using a DDN facility called TELNET. In this scenario, the user enters the DDN through a local host computer that is running the TELNET program (see Figure 6-2).

Each character that you type goes to your local host computer where you can log in as an interactive user. If you now invoke TELNET to establish communication with a remote host computer, TELNET passes your subsequent characters to the local IMP, which places them into a packet and sends the packet out onto the Defense Data Network. The IMP of the remote host computer extracts your characters from the packet and passes them to the remote host computer. Using TELNET, you can extend this process indefinitely, passing characters through one computer after another (each one running the TELNET program) until they finally reach the desired remote host computer.

```
Runs normal
 programs,
like LOGIN                                          Runs TELNET
    |                                                   |
    V                                                   V
-----------     -------         -------   ------------     ------------
| Remote  |     |     |         |     |   | Local    |     | TAC or   |
| Host    |     | IMP |         | IMP |   | Host     |     | Terminal |
| Computer|-----|     |*********|     |---| Computer |***|  or PC   |
-----------     -------    ^    -------   ------------  ^  ------------
 \___ Remote ____/         |     \___ Local ___/        |
                   Long-Distance                  DDN, LAN, or
                   Communication                   Telephone
```

Figure 6–2. TELNET

6.1 The Terminal Access Controller

The Terminal Access Controller (TAC) is a computer which, from the point of view of the DDN, acts like a host computer on the network. The TAC may be either a BBN C/30 computer or a Honeywell 316 computer (the Honeywell 316 is being phased out, and the DDN will soon use BBN C/30's exclusively). The BBN C/30 has 64K bytes of memory and either one or two 32-port asynchronous multiplexors, each of which supports a local console and 31 external terminals or personal computers. The Interface Message Processor (IMP) is a specialized computer that connects a host computer (or a TAC) to the DDN. The functions of the IMP are to collect outgoing characters into packets, which it transmits over the line, and to extract characters and destination addresses from incoming packets. Each IMP can support as many as four host computers and, if these are TACs, it can allow as many as 252 users to access the DDN.

6.2 The Network Virtual Terminal

Fundamental to the operation of the Defense Data Network is the concept of the Network Virtual Terminal (NVT). Many different types of terminals exist today, and they differ in a variety of ways. For instance, some terminals (particularly older ones) are very limited and may support upper-case characters only. On the other hand, some terminals are intelligent and highly specialized—MIT developed an advanced terminal which has a 512-element character set. Some terminals recognize the ASCII (American Standard Code for Information Interchange) character set, while other terminals recognize the EBCDIC (Extended Binary Coded Decimal Interchange Code) character set.

It would be neither logically nor economically feasible to expect every host computer on the Defense Data Network to deal directly with all the different types of computer terminals, each with its own set of characteristics. Instead, each host computer deals with a single, imaginary terminal called a Network Virtual Terminal (NVT). One of the functions of the TAC is to translate character codes emitted by a user's terminal into the equivalent character codes supported by the Network Virtual Terminal. The TAC also translates NVT characters received from the remote host computer into the equivalent characters recognized by the addressee's terminal. The NVT character set includes the full ASCII character set (128 characters), as well as a few special control keys, such as the "BREAK" key, which are not in the full ASCII character set.

6.3

TAC Command Syntax and Interception

The TAC identifies the type of terminal you are using and translates all the characters you type into the NVT character set. In addition the TAC continually looks for special commands (usually consisting of a leading "@" character followed by a string of characters) from the user. These commands configure various aspects of the TAC's operation, such as commanding the TAC to open or close a connection with a remote host computer, commanding the TAC to provide a local echo of the user's characters, and commanding the TAC to collect the characters you type into packets of N characters before transmission.

To distinguish TAC commands from text, you begin each TAC command string with the *Intercept Character*. By default, the intercept character is the atsign (@) character. A typical TAC command is "@ OPEN 99," which opens a connection to IMP number 99. Each TAC command starts with the intercept character and ends either with a linefeed (or carriage return), or with a rubout (the DEL or DELETE key on most keyboards). Termination by a linefeed or carriage return indicates that the TAC should go ahead and process the command. Termination by a rubout indicates that the command should be aborted. The only exception to this rule is the escape sequence of two consecutive intercept characters (@@), which inserts a single intercept character (@) into the character stream which is sent to the remote host computer. TAC commands may occur anywhere in the character stream from the user; they need not start at the beginning of a line. The case of the letters is not important.

Between the intercept character and the linefeed you place one or more words that identify the command. You can abbreviate each word to its first letter, so

@ OPEN 99 -and- @ O 99

are the same command. If a command contains more than one word, then you must separate each word by one or more spaces. There may be zero or more spaces between the intercept character and the first word of the command. For example, the following are equivalent commands:

```
@     BINARY INPUT START
@BINARY INPUT START
@     B I S
@B I     S
```

(this command instructs the TAC to accept 8-bit binary input). Note that the command words *must* be separated by one or more spaces. The command "@BIS" is not valid.

WARNING: Once you start typing the parameters of a command, you destroy any previous parameter values associated with this command, and you can't recover them by aborting the command with a rubout.

You can change any parameter at any time at your terminal, with the exception of some connection parameters while a connection is open (such as trying to open a connection to IMP 50 while the connection to IMP 99 is already open). You'll receive the simple error message "Can't" whenever you attempt an illegal operation of this kind.

A variation in the command format is to place a number between the intercept character and the first word of the command. The number instructs the TAC to perform the command on the corresponding port of your local TAC rather than on the port to which your terminal is attached. This is useful for cases where a shared printer is attached to a TAC rather than to a bidirectional terminal. An example of such a command is:

@23 DEVICE CODE ASCII

In this case, the command "DEVICE CODE ASCII" is directed to port number 23 on your TAC.

6.4

Changing the Intercept Character

The atsign (@) is the default Intercept Character recognized by the TAC. In some cases, this choice may be inconvenient (such as when you must frequently type the atsign as input to the remote host computer). The "@INTERCEPT" command allows you to change the Intercept Character at any time. This command has the following forms:

FULL	*ABBREVIATED*
@ INTERCEPT punct_character	@ I punctuation_character
@ INTERCEPT decimal_number	@ I decimal_number
@ INTERCEPT ESC	@ I E
@ INTERCEPT NONE	@ I N

If you issue this command but do not type a valid decimal number, a character string beginning with the letter "E" or "N", or a punctuation character, then the TAC will respond with the error message "Num" and reset the intercept character to the atsign. Examples of valid "@INTERCEPT" commands are:

```
@I #
@I 42   – 42 is the character "*"
@I E    – "@" becomes the intercept character
```

6.5

Communicating Through a TAC

If you wish to communicate with host computers on the Defense Data Network through a TAC, you must follow a few basic steps in order to establish the connection:

1. Electronically connect to a TAC; in most cases you'll use a modem and dial in via the PSTN (Public Switched Telephone Network).
2. Identify your terminal by striking a specified key before doing anything else.
3. Establish the parameters for the communications link, such as echo control (local or remote).

4. Open up a connection with the host computer (using the "@ OPEN" command).

Once you've opened the connection, you can communicate interactively with the host computer just as if you were directly connected to it.

6.5.1 Connecting to a TAC

The type of connection existing between a terminal and a TAC depends largely on the distance between them. If the terminal is very close (less than 500 feet), the connection may be a simple twisted-pair cable, directly connected to the terminal at one end and to a serial port on the TAC at the other end. For longer distances within the same site, there will be a modem at each end of the cable. If the TAC serves many off-site users, it's more likely that the TAC will have two or three modems, each of which automatically answers a number on the PSTN, and users will dial in by means of a telephone (for a simple terminal) or the communications software (in the case of a personal computer).

Some installations also provide direct connection to TACs or host computers via local area networks. Again, your local support personnel should be able to provide the necessary direction.

6.5.2 Identifying the User's Terminal to a TAC

When you first make a connection with a TAC, it is in *hunt* mode so that it can analyze the first character you send, and thereby determine what baud rate and character set you are using. For this reason, the very first key you strike must always be Control-Q—that is, you hold down the CTRL (Control) key and then strike the Q key at the same time (it doesn't matter whether or not the SHIFT or SHIFT LOCK keys are pressed). If you're connected via a direct cable, it may be necessary for you to strike the BREAK key *before* striking Control-Q. Once the TAC recognizes the Control-Q, it will send you a "herald" message, which usually includes the name of the TAC's site, the version number of the TAC software, and the port number on the TAC to which the user is connected.

If your screen displays the herald message, the TAC port is set to the correct baud rate for your terminal and you may then proceed to open a connection to the desired host computer. If you see a garbled message or nothing, then the terminal and the port are probably set at different baud rates. Most TAC ports are hunting ports (determining the baud rate of the user's terminal from the Control-Q), but some TAC ports are preset to a specific baud rate and do not hunt. The site liaison personnel are responsible for such assignments and you should contact them if you have difficulty in establishing a connection.

If you have difficulty in making a connection, try striking the BREAK key. BREAK puts the port (if it is a hunting port) into hunting mode. Then type the Control-Q. The TAC can hunt to any standard transmission rate from 110 to 9600 bps (bits per second); he standard rates are shown in Figure 6-3. The term "baud" is commonly (but erroneously) used as a synonym for "bps"; in fact, the baud rate is equivalent to bits per second only at speeds below 1200 bps. However, "baud" and "baud rate" are used here because they are so widespread and often appear as designations on equipment panels. Once connected to a TAC, you may use the DEVICE RATE command to change either the baud rate of the port to which you are connected or that of another port on the TAC (if you have the privilege); the DEVICE RATE command is of the form:

@ DEVICE RATE #

or @port DEVICE RATE #

where "port" is the optional decimal port number on the TAC if you are setting the baud rate for another port, and # is one of the values given in Figure 6-3.

#	*Baud Rate*	
178	110	baud
243	134.5	baud
308	150	baud
373	300	baud
438	600	baud
503	1200	baud
568	1800	baud
633	2400	baud
698	4800	baud
763	9600	baud

Figure 6–3. @DEVICE RATE Baud Rate Parameters

Some terminals need delays to be inserted at the end of lines in order not to lose characters when running at high speed. The commands

@ DEVICE CODE EXTRA-PADDING

@ DEVICE CODE OTHER-PADDING

instructs the TAC to insert delays. "@D C E" inserts delays for terminals with slow carriage returns, outputting nulls after each carriage return code; "@D C O" inserts delays appropriate for line printers. The command

@ DEVICE CODE ASCII

removes all padding characters/delays. You can also issue the command @ DEVICE CODE 37

which sets the port for even parity. To change any of the padding or parity settings, you must first reset the port with a "@D C A" command and then issue a new delay or parity command.

6.5.3

Establishing Communications Parameters

Two basic questions must be answered in establishing the communications parameters: (1) how often should messages be transmitted from the TAC/IMP and (2) how should echoing be done. A first-time user can usually ignore both of these questions because the defaults set by the TAC are adequate for the needs of most users. However, as you grow more experienced and want to perform more complex operations, you may need to change the values of some or all the communications parameters; in that case you'll need to learn some new commands and understand their implications.

Each message contains zero or more characters in a packet that is generated by the Interface Message Processor (IMP). By default, the TAC sends one character per packet. This is a simple but very inefficient mechanism since each packet has at least 60 bytes of addressing and error detection information as well. In some cases, it is more advantageous to select one of the other techniques:

@TRANSMIT NOW
- transmit what has been collected so far

@TRANSMIT ON MESSAGE-END
- transmit when an ASCII DC3 (Control-S) is sent by the terminal

@TRANSMIT ON LINEFEED
- transmit when a linefeed character is sent by the terminal

@TRANSMIT EVERY N
- transmit every N chars or as close to N as the TAC's buffers will allow; N is a decimal number

@TRANSMIT EVERY O
- (O is the letter "O") resets the "@T O M" and "@T O L" modes

The command "@T E 0" (Transmit on Every 0) resets the TAC to its original state of transmitting one character per packet.

If the TAC's buffer contains characters that you don't wish to transmit to the host, you can clear the TAC's input buffers of all unsent characters with the command:

@FLUSH

When you press the RETURN key, the terminal sends only a carriage return character; however, the TAC must send the host a linefeed or null character, as well. The default is for the TAC to insert a linefeed character (which also marks the termination of a TAC command). The following commands explicitly control linefeed and null character insertion:

@ INSERT LINEFEED
  – insert linefeed after carriage return
@ CLEAR INSERT LINEFEED
  – insert null after carriage return

When you strike a key on the keyboard, you want the corresponding character to appear on your screen so that you can be sure you pressed the correct key; therefore, every character that you send is echoed back to your screen from one of three places: (1) the user's terminal, (2) the TAC, and (3) the remote host computer. You can select the point at which the echo occurs by issuing one of these commands:

@ ECHO HALFDUPLEX
  – echo at the terminal
@ ECHO LOCAL or ALL
  – echo at the TAC
@ ECHO REMOTE or NONE
  – echo at the remote host

Each of these commands sets the TAC to the correct echo mode (echo, or no echo) and, if the connection is open at the time, the TAC in turn transmits a command that requests the remote host also to enter the proper echo mode.

6.5.4 Opening and Closing Connections with Host Computers

Three commands are of particular interest because they open and close connections with remote host computers:

@ OPEN N
  – open connection with host on IMP N
@ CLOSE
  – close the current connection
@ RESET
  – reset the current connection

The "@ C" command closes the TAC connection to the current remote host computer. The TAC port is now idle and ready to receive another command.

The "@ R" command resets the current TAC connection. Any existing connections are closed, terminal parameters are reset to their preset values, and the TAC will display its herald. This command does not return the port to its hunting state (if it is a hunting port), but leaves the TAC ready for another command. In full, the "@ R" command does the following:

1. Does a "give back" on the user's port;
2. Returns echo mode to LOCAL ECHO with REMOTE ECHO desired (and requested once a connection is made);
3. Sets the port to allow 8-bit binary mode when requested;
4. Sets transmission mode to "@T E 0", so every character is placed into its own packet;
5. Sets "wild" mode to not wild; and
6. Inserts linefeed after carriage return;

The "@ R" command does not change the DEVICE RATE setting and does not alter flow control, padding, or parity for the port.

The "@ O" command opens a connection between a remote host computer and the user's TAC. The number associated with the "@ OPEN" command is the number identifying the desired remote host computer. This number may take one of two basic forms:

net:host/imp;port (like 26:3/99;4)

or

net.host.lhost.imp;port (like 26.3.0.99;4)

If the computer is on the same network as the user, the net number may be omitted. If the host is host computer 0, then the host number may be omitted. The port number is not usually of interest to the casual user and may be omitted; its default value is 23 (decimal). Only the imp number is required, and, for most addresses, only the imp number is needed. Examples:

1. a single number, like "99" which refers to host number 0 on IMP number 99 (an IMP can

typically support up to four host computers, numbered 0 to 3) on the same network as the user's TAC

2. number/number, like "1/99" which refers to host number 1 on IMP number 99 on the same network as the user's TAC
3. the full network address, like "10.1.0.99" which refers to host number 1 on IMP number 99 on network number 10 (the field containing the 0 in this example is a logical host number and is usually 0)

6.5.4.1

Address Form 1

Address Form 1 is:

net:host/imp;port

where

NET is the number of the network to which the remote host computer is connected. This decimal number can take on values from 0 to 255. The default value (if this field is omitted) is the network on which the user's TAC resides.

HOST is the number of the port of the IMP to which the remote host computer is attached. While most IMPs can only connect to four host computers, the value of the host field is a decimal number from 0 to 255. If not specified, the default value is 0.

IMP is the IMP number to which the remote host computer is connected. This decimal number can range from 0 to 65,535, and it has no default value (the IMP number must be specified).

PORT is the number of the port to which the TAC will connect. This decimal number can range from 0 to 65,535, and it defaults to the new Telnet socket (23 decimal).

6.5.4.2

Address Form 2

Address Form 2 is:

net.host.lhost.imp;port

where

The values for *NET*, *HOST*, *IMP*, and *PORT* are the same as those described above.

LHOST is a logical host number, and its default value is 0. This number is used on some networks.

6.5.4.3

Host Computer Addressing

The full address of a host computer (less the port number) is made up of net.host.lhost.imp, and it comprises a 32-bit internet address. Each host on the DDN has a unique 32-bit internet address, so the DDN provides complete addressability and interoperability between its host computers (including its TACs). This also means that each packet placed on the net by a TAC or host computer must contain a 32-bit internet address for the packet's source address and a 32-bit internet address for the packet's destination address as well as other information in the packet overhead. Hence, in order for the TAC to transmit one character to a remote host computer (when the TAC is in the "@T E 1" mode), over 64 bits of packet overhead are generated by the IMP.

As can be guessed by this form of address, the Defense Data Network is set up to support more exotic operations than simply connecting users with host computers. Host computers can be connected with other host computers (which is where the File Transfer Protocol, FTP, frequently comes into play), and users can be connected with other users. Details of how a user can manually make such interconnections via the TACs are outside the scope of this book, and the reader is referred to the documents described in the "Further Reading" appendix.

6.5.4.4

Network Numbers

The MILNET, on which SIMTEL20 resides, is network number 26. The ARPANET is network number 10. MINET, the Military Intelligence network, is network number 24.

Network number 128 is actually the base address for over a hundred other networks. Each of these networks is identified in the host computer field. For instance, 128.2.x.x refers to hosts on CMU-NET (at Carnegie-Mellon University), 128.6.x.x is RUTGERS, and 128.30, 128.31, and 128.52 are at MIT.

Network number 192 is for yet another group of networks, and the addressing scheme is different from network number 128. For instance, 192.5.88.x is at Yale, while 192.5.89.x is at Harvard.

How many computer networks comprise the Defense Data Network? Over 400!

6.5.5

TAC Login

After you've established communication with a TAC, the TAC will prompt you for a user ID and password when you first attempt to open a connection to a host computer (see Figure 6-4). All registered DDN users are given a TAC user ID and password by the DDN Network Information Center, and accessing the DDN through a TAC requires knowledge of both the proper telephone numbers and a user ID and password. Once the TAC has accepted your user ID and password, it won't prompt you again for this information during the rest of the session unless you issue the "@ L" command. The command:

@ LOGOUT

logs you out of the TAC and you'll have to provide your user ID and password the next time you issue an "@ O" command to the TAC.

```
^Q
WELCOME TO DDN.
**FOR OFFICIAL USE ONLY**
TAC LOGIN REQUIRED
CALL NIC 1-800-235-3155 FOR HELP
type @n for news.
ABER TAC 113 #:04
@o 74

TAC Userid: MYID
Access Code:

Login OK
TCP Trying...Open
Report any problems to ACTION@SIMTEL20

Welcome to SIMTEL20, TOPS-20 Monitor 5.4(1044)-4
The system has been up for 1 day, 16 hours and 10 minutes
There are 4+6 jobs and the load average is  4.05
@mylogin
Job 19 on TTY72 22-Oct-86 12:13AM
Previous LOGIN: 20-Oct-86 10:17AM
End of LOGIN.CMD.14
```

Figure 6–4. TAC Login Procedure

The *TAC Access Control System* (TACACS) validates user IDs and passwords and provides an online data base tool which allows a user to change his password and, if he has the proper authorization, to add new users. The TACACS data base maintenance tool is accessed through the DDN via the special command:

@ U

The TAC must be idle (ie, not connected to a particular host computer), and the "@ U" command connects the user to the TACACS computer, placing him at the prompt:

TACAC>

To use the tool, the user must first login by supplying the user ID and password he uses to login to the TAC. The command is:

LOGIN USER_ID

and the user will be prompted for the password.

User passwords are generated by the database tool at the TACACS. A password is between 8 and 12 characters long and has an expiration date, which is usually 180 days from the day it was created or last changed.

The user can obtain a new password from the TACACS by issuing the command:

GET-NEW-PASSWORD

The operation is self-explanatory from there.

Online help is available through the DESCRIBE command. The form:

DESCRIBE ?

prints a list of available commands, and the form:

DESCRIBE TOPIC

(where TOPIC is an available command) documents the use of a particular command in detail.

6.5.6 Other TAC Commands

The TAC also recognizes many other commands. For reference, some of these commands are presented in Figure 6-4. The "Further Reading" appendix points to where more details can be found.

@ Command	*Brief Description*
CLEAR DEVICE WILD	Set device to be unwild
# DIVERT OUTPUT	Capture device # and divert this terminal's output to it.
# GIVE BACK	Release control of captured device #
HOST #	Simultaneous "@S T H" and "@R F H"
INITIAL CONNECTION PROTOCOL	Start the initial connection protocol
M # #	Mag tape command # with argument #
PROTOCOL BOTH	Simultaneous "@P T T" and "@P T R"
PROTOCOL TO RECEIVE	Manually initiate connection protocol
PROTOCOL TO TRANSMIT	Manually initiate connection protocol
RECEIVE FROM HOST #	Establish Host # parameter for manual initialization
RECEIVE FROM SOCKET #	Establish socket # parameter for manual initialization of connection
RECEIVE FROM WILD	Equivalent to "@R F S <any>"
SEND BREAK	Send the Telnet "BREAK" character
SEND COMMAND	Send the command escape character
SEND SYNC	Send the Telnet "SYNC" character and an "INTERRUPT SENDER" message
SEND TO HOST #	Establish Host # parameter for manual initialization of connection
SEND TO SOCKET #	Establish socket # parameter for manual initialization of connection
SEND TO WILD	Equivalent to "@S T S <any>"

Figure 6-5. Other TAC Commands

6.5.7

Selected TAC Error Messages

The following are selected error messages which may be displayed to the user by the TAC. The "Further Reading" appendix points to material which can provide a complete list of TAC error messages. Some selected TAC error messages are presented in Figure 6-5.

TAC Error Message	*Meaning*
BAD	The TAC does not recognize the command
Can't	The TAC is already connected to a remote host computer, and the user must close or reset the connection before making an attempt to connect to another host
Closed	Connection closed
Connection Restored	Destination IMP has restored the connection as it was before the IMP or its host halted
Destination host dead	The Destination Host is not communicating with the network
Destination unreachable	There is no path from the TAC to the Destination Host through the communications network
Host Broke the Connection	The Destination Host's service is restored but all network tables have been reset
Host closing connection	The remote host has closed its connection to the TAC; the TAC port is idle
Host not responding	Destination Host is not up from the point of view of the network
Host Scheduled Down Until ...	Destination Host is scheduled down until the date and time indicated
Host Unscheduled Down Until ...	Destination Host is unscheduled down until the date and time indicated
Net Trouble	Destination IMP cannot be reached due to some kind of trouble with the network
NO	Parameters may not be set for specified terminal
Num	The TAC expected a number; command terminated
Open	Connection opened
Refused	The remote host rejected the attempt to establish connection
TAC'S IMP Down	The IMP which connects the TAC to the DDN is down, so the TAC is isolated
Trying ...	The TAC/IMP is now servicing the user's OPEN request
Wait	The TAC is attempting to contact RSEXEC Server (details on what an RSEXEC Server is are outside the scope of this book)

Figure 6–6. Selected TAC Error Messages

Chapter 7

Microcomputer Communications Protocols

After transferring files from a remote DDN host computer to your local host, usually with the aid of FTP, you may want to transfer some or all of these files from your local host to your personal computer (PC), either for actual use there, or for distribution to other PCs by various means. This chapter discusses the most common communications protocols that let you transfer files from mainframes to PCs and vice versa, and between PCs.

7.1 Christensen Protocol—Mainframe Programs

For a microcomputer to exchange files reliably with a mainframe, both machines must run cooperating file transfer programs that provide automatic error detection and retransmission of faulty blocks. One family of such programs uses a popular protocol (called XMODEM) created by Ward Christensen for PC-to-PC file transfers, and enhanced by others with improved error-detection mechanisms. The family now includes XMODEM programs that run on mainframes.

Vendors of commercial telecommunications software have a nasty habit of stating that their proprietary protocols are "far more reliable than XMODEM." Those statements are true in so far as very early versions of XMODEM are concerned, because they used a checksum error-detection algorithm that detects no more than 99 percent of all transmission errors. Some vendors who claim to support XMODEM, in fact support only the checksum algorithm. The enhanced versions, current since 1982, use a cyclic redundancy check that detects 99.988 percent of all errors and is surpassed only by the adaptive detection mechanisms embodied in the hardware of very recent high-speed modems. If you are using an XMODEM program that supports CRC error detection, you don't need to worry much about the possibility of undetected errors in your file transfers.

Directory PD:<UNIX.CPM> contains two programs, UC and the older UMODEM (both written in C), which implement the XMODEM protocol on UNIX machines. See the file PD:<UNIX>UNIX.CRCLST for a list of other useful UNIX utilities; some of these files and utilities are shown in Figure 7-1.

PD:<UNIX.CPM>	
AUTOFTP.DOC	Notes on automatic file transfers via FTP
COMHEX.C	Program to convert binary files (COM files)
.MAN	to Intel Hex files (text form) and manual
CRCK2.C	Program to compute CRC values for file
.MAN	and manual
LAR.C	Library archival program
TMODEM.C	A modem program
.MAN	and manual
UC13.MAN	Manual for the UC modem program
UC16.C	The UC modem program
UMODEM35.MAN	Manual for the UMODEM modem program
UMODEM37.C	The UMODEM modem program
XSQ107.C	File squeezing program
XUSQ107.C	File unsqueezing program

Figure 7-1. Selected UNIX/C Programs

On ITS machines (such as MIT-MC and other members of the local computing environment at MIT), file transfer using the Christensen protocol can be done using MMODEM (type ":MMODEM" for instructions), or LMODEM. Documentation for LMODEM is in a file named .INFO.;LMODEM HELP on MIT-MC and other hosts at MIT. Other useful ITS utilities include those listed in Figure 7-2.

TYPE8	–	types an ASCII file stored in ITS binary format.
TYPESQ	–	types an ITS binary format "squeezed" file (see the first paragraph under FILE TYPES).
USQ	–	creates an unsqueezed version of a squeezed file.
HEXIFY	–	creates an Intel hex format file from an ITS binary format COM file.
COMIFY	–	creates a COM file from an Intel hex file.
CRC	–	computes the Cyclic Redundancy Check value for a file, using the same algorithm that is used by the CP/M program CRCK.

Figure 7–2. Selected ITS Programs

Brief instructions for any of these utilities except LMODEM can be obtained by typing ":utility_name" (for example, :CRC to obtain the instructions for use of the Cyclic Redundancy Check program).

The ITS utilities listed above are also available for use with TOPS-20, and these utilities have been converted to work with TOPS-20 binary formats. A collection of TOPS-20 utilities for transferring and manipulating files which are companions to those used on CP/M systems can be found in directory PD:<MISC.TOPS-20>. See PD:<MISC>MISC.CRCLST for a list of available programs in this subdirectory. A few of these files are shown in Figure 7-3.

File transfer and conversion utilities for use on VAX/VMS machines are contained in directory PD:<MISC.VAXVMS>. Like the programs in PD:<MISC.TOPS-20>, these are companions to those used on CP/M systems. A few of these files are shown in Figure 7-4.

PD:<MISC.TOPS-20>	
DE-LBR.EXE	Program to extract files from LBR files
.MID	and source code
HEXIFY.EXE	Program to create Intel Hex files
.HLP	
.MAC	
MAKLBR.EXE	Program to create LBR files under TOPS-20
.MID	
.MSG	
NCRC.EXE	Program to compute CRC values
.MID	
TMODEM.MAC	A modem program, compatible with XMODEM
USQ.EXE	File unsqueezing program
.MID	

Figure 7–3. Selected TOPS-20 Programs

PD:<MISC.VAXVMS>	
VMSDEH.MAR	Program to convert hex to binary
VMSHEX.MAR	Program to convert binary to hex
VVMODEM.C	A modem program
XMODEM.COM	An implementation of XMODEM for
.DOC	VAX/VMS
.HLP	
.MSG	
.NOTE	
XMODEM54.FOR	

Figure 7–4. Selected VMS Programs

7.2

Christensen Protocol—Microcomputer Programs

An excellent program for transferring files between micros or between micros and mainframes is called MODM7xx, where the "xx" is replaced with two digits representing the current version. This program, often referred to as MODEM7,uses the popular Christensen protocol to transfer files with automatic CRC error detection and retransmission of erroneous blocks. The directory PD:<CPM.MODEM7> contains the files associated with MODM7xx.

MEX stands for "Modem EXecutive", and it is a communications and file transfer program with a built-in mini operating system that runs under CP/M or MSDOS. MEX can transfer files using either the Christensen or Compuserve protocol. It has an enormous potential for highly automated operations because it can read and execute command-scripts pre-stored in disk files. These scripts can, for example, send commands to a remote computer just as if they had been sent manually from the microcomputer in terminal-mode. Users of this relatively new program are still exploring its possibilities. For more information, look in CPM.CRCLST under the heading "PD:<CPM.MEX>", and then get the various files that have "DQC" and "IQF" in their names. These DOCumentation and INFormation files are stored in squeezed form (note the "Q" in the filename extensions), so you will have to unsqueeze them (by using USQ or equivalent). Overlays for MODM7xx (which are used to customize MODM7xx for use on a particular computer) will also work with MEX, but they won't provide all of the extended MEX features.

7.3 Kermit

Another excellent program for transferring files is called Kermit. This program has the advantage of being available for an impressively large number of mainframes and micros. It is, for example, available for the IBM-PC, CP/M, UNIX, TOPS-20, and VMS, and it does not require CP/M or 8-bit character codes.

To get started with KERMIT, connect to the Kermit archive host computer at Columbia University, CU20B.ARPA, and, using FTP, give the command:

get ker:aaaread.me

The name of this file is subject to change. If you cannot find a file with this name, snoop around in the first half dozen or so files in the alphabetical listing obtainable using the FTP DIR command. You should find something useful.

Questions can be addressed to INFO-KERMIT-REQUEST at CU20B.ARPA.

7.4

Getting Started

In order to get MODM7xx, MEX or Kermit running on your microcomputer, you must first transfer the necessary files from an archive mainframe (such as SIMTEL20.ARPA or CU20B.ARPA) to your microcomputer. If you already have a capture-to-disk communications program of some sort, you can use it to move the needed files. In the long run, you'll have to have the ability to transfer 8-bit binary files, but initially most of what you need will be in text files. Some of the files are quite large. For example, MODM7xx.COM is over 18K bytes, and the HEX file (which you will need if you can't transfer 8-bit files) is over 45K. Moving large files to your micro without using an error detecting protocol can result in frustrating errors. You can elimitate most of these by obtaining multiple copies of each file and then performing manual or machine-assisted comparisons of the versions to locate and repair bad parts of the code. However, there is a better way.

Directory PD:<CPM.STARTER-KIT> contains a short starter program called PIPMODEM.ASM. Transfer this program to your your local host, using FTP, and print it. Then enter the source code into your microcomputer by hand and assemble it. You can then use PIPMODEM to down-load either MBOOT3.ASM or BMODEM.BAS (depending on whether you prefer assembly language or BASIC), both of which can receive files using the error-detecting Christensen protocol. Once you have this capability, you can download the full-function file transfer program of your choice. To examine this option, connect to SIMTEL20 via FTP and give the commands:

```
get pd:<cpm.starter-kit>pipmodem.asm
get pd:<cpm.starter-kit>pipmodem.doc
get pd:<cpm.starter-kit>mboot3.asm
get pd:<cpm.starter-kit>bmodem.bas
```

get pd:<cpm.starter-kit>bmodem.doc

All are ASCII text files. Read PIPMODEM.DOC first, then look at MBOOT3.ASM and BMODEM.DOC. PIPMODEM.DOC explains the situation very nicely. If you have any questions about these programs, send them to INFO-CPM@AMSAA.ARPA (*not* to INFO-CPM-REQUEST).

SECTION II: THE SIMTEL20 HOST COMPUTER

– Outline –

Notes

Chapter 8

History of the Repositories

On August 29, 1979, the INFO-CPM electronic mailing list was formed as a spin-off of the INFO-MICRO electronic mailing list. Both lists were based at the MIT-MC host computer on the ARPANET (at this time, MIT-MC was the host computer for the MACSYMA Consortium research project at the Massachusetts Institute of Technology). In September, members of INFO-CPM discovered Keith Petersen's Royal Oak RCP/M system, and Keith was invited to participate directly in the INFO-CPM discussions. Keith was given an account on MIT-MC, and he started uploading software from his RCP/M system to MIT-MC for further distribution through the ARPANET. The INFO-CPM electronic mailing list was used to announce new files as they were uploaded to MIT-MC, and thus the first repository, a collection of CP/M software, was born.

Several mainframe versions of CP/M utilities were gradually developed. LMODEM, the first mainframe implementation of the Christensen Protocol, was written in MacLISP by Ed Barton. Gail Zacharias developed MMODEM, USQ, HEXIFY, COMIFY, MAKLBR, DE-LBR, and other tools, some of which were modified for use on TOPS-20 systems. Bill Westfield wrote the original MODEM program for TOPS-20, which has since been modified into the TMODEM program.

Disk space was limited on MIT-MC, and, when the MACSYMA Consortium was dissolved in September 1983, SIMTEL20 (SIMulation and TELeprocessing DECSYSTEM-20) at White Sands Missile Range (WSMR) in New Mexico had come online with disk space to spare. During September, the CP/M repository was moved from MIT-MC to SIMTEL20.

The DARCOM Microcomputer Software Sharing System (DMSSS) had also purchased the entire CPMUG, SIG/M, and PC/BLUE collections of public domain software, and these collections became three more repositories on SIMTEL20. SIMTEL20 has since been added to the SIG/M and PC/BLUE regional distributions, and these bodies of software are constantly being updated on SIMTEL20.

It soon became evident that a collection of UNIX/C versions of the CP/M utilities would be required to support the growing UNIX community on the Defense Data Network, and the UNIX archive was formed. The Logistics Systems Support Activity (LSSA) of the Army Materiel Command (AMC) sponsored the UNIX archive, providing funds for the disk structure known today as PD:. In November, 1985, all repositories were moved to PD:.

In November 1984, Richard Conn felt that there existed a need to establish a repository of Ada software and, with the encouragement and sponsorship of Frank Wancho, Richard formed the Ada Software Repository (ASR) and the ADA-SW electronic mailing list over which users of the ASR could communicate with each other.

The CPM repository became the collection of the latest versions of CP/M software, and another archive, MSDOS, was created to contain the latest versions of PC/BLUE software for the IBM PC and its compatibles. The INFO-IBMPC collections on USC-ISIB (University of Southern California, Information Sciences Institute System B) and Pete Galvin's collection on UTEXAS-20 (University of Texas) were merged into MSDOS.

The ZSYS archive was later added to support users of ZCPR3 and its derivative, Richard Conn's Z System. Additionally, a new top-level directory called MISC was created containing software not falling under the other repositories. There are now nine repositories on SIMTEL20: CPM, SIGM, CPMUG, PC-BLUE, MSDOS, UNIX, ZSYS, ADA, and MISC.

As the subscription list to INFO-CPM grew, it was gatewayed into the USENET community, first as fa.info-cpm, and then as a two-way newsgroup, net.micro.cpm, which it is today. Later, members of other networks such as CSNET, BITNET, and others joined the list. As new files were added to the CPM repository and announcements made to INFO-CPM, users from the other communities became frustrated because access to these files was limited to those with Internet FTP access to SIMTEL20 (those directly on the Defense Data Network).

To address this need, the concept of the Archive Server was born around July 1986. The original concept for the Archive Server came from a mail file server developed by Jack Dongarra of the Argonne National Laboratory and Eric Grosse of AT&T Bell Laboratories. The mail file server, called NetLib, was made available on ANL-MCS (at Argonne National Laboratory) to permit mail access to its collection of public domain mathematic software routines. The development of NetLib was supported in part by the National Science Foundation (NSF).

The Archive Server on SIMTEL20 has recently become operational, having been beta tested by Matt Kimmel on the BITNET and Eric Hildum on the USENET. Any user on any network connected to the Defense Data Network can now access all of the repositories on SIMTEL20 by using the Archive Server. Details on accessing and using the Archive Server are presented in another section of this book.

Chapter 9

SIMTEL20 and The TOPS-20 Operating System

The Ada Software Repository (ASR) is stored on a DEC-20 mainframe computer called SIMTEL20 which is running the TOPS-20 operating system. Both the computer and operating system are products of Digital Equipment Corporation. This chapter presents a brief overview of TOPS-20 which is targeted directly to the users of the ASR and the other repositories on SIMTEL20.

9.1 Directory and File Names

All programs, text, and data are stored in files, and each file has a label or file specification (*filespec* for short). Files are stored in groups called *directories*.

For our purposes, a filespec has the form:

device:<directory>filename.filetype.generation

or

device:<directory.subdirectory>filename.filetype.generation

where *device:* is the name of the physical device on which the file resides, *<directory>* is the name of the directory in which the file resides and *<directory.subdirectory>* is the full name of the subdirectory in which the file resides, *filename.filetype* is the name and type of the file, and *generation* is the generation, or version, number of the file. Examples of filespecs are:

PD:<ADA>ADA.CRCLST.25762
PD:<ADA.POINTERS>COMPILERS.INF.88
PD:<ADA.COMPONENTS>DSTR1.SRC.2

The TOPS-20 operating system simplifies the overhead of referring to a file by allowing certain defaults to take effect if a particular part of a filespec is omitted by the user. If the "device:" field is omitted, the connected structure (the device into which the user is logged at the time) is assumed.

If the "<directory>" field is omitted, the connected directory (the directory into which the user is logged at the time) is assumed. Most FTP servers allow the user to issue a "CD" or "CWD" (change directory or change working directory) command, and this command specifies a connected structure or connected directory. The CD command usually takes the form:

CD device:<directory>

Two device names are frequently employed by users of SIMTEL20. They are PS: (which stands for Public Structure) and PD: (which stands for Public Domain). The PD: device is a 512M-byte disk drive (at the time of this writing) which holds all of the repositories on SIMTEL20. The PS: device (176M bytes) contains some specialized directories which are mentioned from time to time.

A directory name, specified by "<directory>", can indicate a single top-level directory or a directory subtree (in which one directory, called a *subdirectory*, is stored within another directory). Directory references usually take forms like:

<directory>
<directory.subdirectory>
<directory.subdirectory.subdirectory>

By convention, the repositories on SIMTEL20 go no deeper than one subdirectory, and the top-level directory name is the name of the repository itself. For example:

<ADA>
is the Ada Software Repository
<ADA.EDUCATION>
is the EDUCATION subdirectory of ADA
<SIGM>

is the SIG/M Repository
<SIGM.VAXVMS>
is the VAX/VMS subdirectory of SIGM

The "generation" field is the generation, or version, number of the file. If omitted, the highest generation (largest generation number) is selected.

The "filename" and "filetype" fields are the characters of the file's name, and TOPS-20 allows both of these fields to be quite long. The various repositories place restrictions on the lengths of these fields, depending on the intended audiences. The SIGM repository, for instance, requires the filename field to be no longer than eight characters and the filetype field to be no longer than three characters. This is because the users of SIGM are employing CP/M or compatible operating systems which enforce these constraints. In the case of the Ada Software Repository, the filename field is restricted to nine characters (the first six of which must be unique) and the filetype field is restricted to three characters. These restrictions are enforced for two reasons: (1) to allow for a lowest-common-denominator among the various operating systems employed on the Defense Data Network and (2) to prevent file name conflicts when tapes are made using the various tape formats supported by the tape distribution facility at SIMTEL20.

Two characters, called *wildcard* characters, can be included in the directory, filename, and filetype fields of a filespec to support pattern matching when the exact content of the field is not known. Some FTP servers also allow these wildcards to be used, thereby allowing groups of files to be transferred by one command. These wildcard characters are the asterisk (*) and the percent sign (%). The asterisk represents zero or more characters, and the percent sign fills in for a single character. For example, given the files:

FILE1.TXT	FILE1.DOC	FILE1.SRC
FILE2.TXT	FILE3.TXT	MYFILE.DOC

then:

Filespec with Wildcards	*Matches*
FILE1.*	FILE1.TXT, FILE1.DOC, FILE1.SRC

FILE%.TXT	FILE1.TXT, FILE2.TXT, FILE3.TXT
FILE*.*	FILEX.TXT, FILE1.TXT, FILE1.DOC,FILE1.SRC, FILE2.TXT, FILE3.TXT
FILE.DOC	MYFILE.DOC, FILE1.DOC

In the "device:" field, only the asterisk may be used in the following limited sense: "chars*:", as in "P*:" to match "PS:" and "PD:".

In the "generation" field, only the asterisk may be used, and it substitutes for the entire field (eg, FILE1.DOC.*).

9.2

More on TOPS-20 and the SIMTEL20 Repositories

The directory entry for a file contains the filespec and many other fields, such as creation date, last modification date, size, and number of accesses. Tools are available on SIMTEL20 which generate reports and file listings that present information from these fields. In particular, the directory PD:<ADA> contains the file FILEUSE.DOC which contains the filespecs of all files in the Ada Software Repository ordered by number of accesses. Each time a file is accessed on SIMTEL20, the access count field in its directory entry is incremented.

TOPS-20 is a multiuser, multitasking operating system, and tools are available on SIMTEL20 to allow users on the system to monitor the activity of other users. The people who employ FTP to access SIMTEL20 do not have these capabilities, but people who can log directly onto SIMTEL20 can see how many FTP processes are running and other items of information on the activity of the system.

SIMTEL20 supports a wide variety of specialized tools for its users, and many of these tools are available to users on other computers through the repositories on SIMTEL20 and other host computers on the Defense Data Network. Some of the tools maintained on SIMTEL20 include:

1. **TMODEM** – TMODEM is a very efficient implementation of the XMODEM

communications protocol which supports the transfer of both binary and text files in 128-byte or 1K-byte packets between SIMTEL20 and any personal computer (such as an IBM PC or CP/M PC) connected to it. TMODEM cooperates with PCs connected to SIMTEL20 either directly or through the DDN (in the latter case it has to negotiate binary communication with the DDN).

2. **KERMIT** – KERMIT is a less efficient, but more versatile communications protocol than the XMODEM protocol. XMODEM requires 8-bit character codes, whereas KERMIT does not. Thus, you can use KERMIT in a variety of environments (eg, 7-bit local-area networks) in which XMODEM cannot function. The KERMIT implementation on SIMTEL20 can also negotiate a binary communications path on the DDN, allowing it to employ a slightly more efficient transfer mechanism. The KERMIT packet size is restricted to 94 bytes, so KERMIT is still less efficient than XMODEM.

3. **Online Documentation Support** – A host of tools comes into play in documenting the Ada and Z-System Software Repositories. These tools are written in C and TOPS-20 command language, and they provide an automated mechanism for maintaining, tracking, and updating software documentation. This toolset maintains both the on-line data bases and the hard-copy documents generated for these repositories.

4. **File Compression and Decompression Tools** – Implementations of SQ, USQ, UUENCODE, and other file compression and decompression tools are available on SIMTEL20. These tools allow files to be stored in the repositories in compressed forms that you can transfer to your PC and then decompress using local implementations of the same programs. Compressing files saves disk space and reduces transfer time, while retaining all of the information contained in these files. To ensure maximum transportability, the files in the Ada Software Repository are left in conventional text forms, but most of the files in other repositories,

such as SIGM, are stored in compressed forms.

5. **Library Maintenance Tools** – Groups of related files are frequently collected together into one composite file, called a *library file*. SIMTEL20 supports four standards for library files: (1) the LBR format, used mainly by CP/M and MSDOS PC users; (2) the ARC format, used mainly by MSDOS and CP/M PC users (MSDOS more than CP/M); (3) the SHAR (SHell ARchive) format, used mainly by UNIX users; and (4) the PAGER format, used mainly by UNIX and Ada Software Repository users. SIMTEL20 supports a variety of tools that let you manipulate library files in these various formats within the SIMTEL20 environment.

9.3

File Types

Files are stored in one of two formats: Text files, such as those with names ending in DOC, HEX, INF and ASM, are sometimes stored as ASCII files, but usually these files are stored in binary squeezed form. Binary storage is also used for executable (COM) and library files. Squeezed and library files are described below. All binary data are stored as four 8-bit bytes per 36-bit SIMTEL20 word; the four least significant bits of each word are filled with zeros. If such a file is interpreted as a contiguous string, as will happen if a straight binary transfer is made to a 16 or 32-bit UNIX machine, the four zeroed filler bits in each 36-bit group will cause rather bizarre and frustrating results. There are methods for dealing with this situation, which differ from machine to machine; they are generally implemented in a manner that is completely transparent to the user and will not be explained here. However, if you have to know the details, consult your local support personnel.

Squeezed files have been compressed using programs available in directory PD:<CPM.SQUSQ> to obtain a size reduction of approximately 35 percent. These files can be identified by the letter Q in the filetype field. For example, the file PD:<CPM.ASMUTL> RMACPAT.AQM is a squeezed file. You must transfer it as a *binary* file and then unsqueeze it. On a

CP/M system you can do the unsqueezing with USQ-xx.COM (where "xx" is the current version) from directory PD:<CPM.SQUSQ>. Alternatively, you can use one of the host-based unsqueezers in the PD:<CPM> and PD:<UNIX> archives (see for example, directories PD:<MISC.TOPS-20>, PD:<MSDOS.SQ-USQ>, and PD:<UNIX.CPM>).

ABS	– An abstract
ADA	– An Ada program
CMM	– A comment file, which provides additional information on an item of software in the ASR
CO	– A compilation order file, which names the files associated with an item of software in the order in which they should be compiled
COM	– A command file (usually for VAX/VMS)
DAT	– A data file
DIS	– A distribution file, which names the files associated with an item of software
DOC	– A documentation file
INF	– An information file (another name for a DOC file)
ME	– A "read me first" file which should be read before looking at other files associated with an item of software
PRO	– A prologue file, which contains information on the author and public domain release of an item of software in the ASR
PTR	– A pointer file, which contains text that refers to some source outside of the ASR
SRC	– One or more Ada source code files concatenated by the PAGER tool
TST	– A test file, which contains test data or test programs or both

Figure 9-1. File Types Used in the Ada Software Repository

CP/M library files (those with names ending in LBR) combine several regular CP/M files into a single *binary* file that contains an internal directory of its contents. LBR files are created with the aid of the CP/M library utility LUxxx.COM (where "xxx" is the current version) or some other compatible utility. The complete packages for LUxxx and a newer compatible program called NULUxx (where "xx" is the version) can be found in directory PD:<CPM.CPMLIB>. C-language source code for a compatible UNIX utility called LAR (library archiver) is in directory PD:<UNIX.CPM>.

Although the type of storage used for a particular file can usually be inferred from the file name, this is not always true. It is a good idea to check the appropriate "crclst" file to ascertain the storage format used for each file of interest.

Because the repositories on SIMTEL20 consume a large amount of disk space, it's necessary to conserve storage capacity by the greatest possible use of libraries and squeezed files, both of which are stored in binary format.

Several file types have particular meaning in conjunction with the Ada Software Repository. These file types are presented in Figure 9-1.

9.4

CRCLST Files

Each repository has files in its top level directory called CRCLST files:

pd:<ada>ada.crclst
pd:<cpm>cpm.crclst
pd:<cpmug>cpmug.crclst
pd:<msdos>msdos.crclst
pd:<pc-blue>pc-blue.crclst
pd:<sigm>sigm.crclst
pd:<unix>unix.crclst
pd:<zsys>zsys.crclst
pd:<misc>misc.crclst

These are text files that contain directory listings of their respective repositories. The <CPM> repository contains the latest CP/M offerings, and is updated frequently. The <CPMUG>, <SIGM> and <PC-BLUE> repositories contain software distributed by the CP/M Users Group, the SIG/M Users Group and the PC-Blue Users Group respectively. This software is available on diskettes from the associated users groups, and the repositories are updated as new volumes are issued. The <PC-BLUE> repository contains software for the IBM-PC and similar machines. Some software runs under CP/M, and some software runs under PCDOS/MSDOS. The <MSDOS> repository also contains software for the MSDOS and PCDOS operating systems; but this repository is locally managed, and therefore is updated more frequently than the <PC-BLUE> repository. The <UNIX> repository contains a variety of UNIX tools. Those which apply specifically to CP/M are in the directory <UNIX.CPM>. The <ADA> repository is growing rapidly. Information about this repository is in directory PD:<ADA.GENERAL>. The <ZSYS> repository contains files of interest to users of ZCPR3 and the Z System associated with ZCPR3.

Because of the large number of files available, the repository maintainers cannot possibly attempt to validate the proper operation of the various programs. When a program bug is reported, immediate action is taken to either correct the error or remove the offending program from the repositories. Still, users must understand that all archive programs are offered AS IS, and the archive maintainers specifically disclaim any liability should these programs malfunction or cause damage, incidental or otherwise. When testing any new software, be certain that all information stored on disk is backed up before starting, so that recovery is simplified if files are damaged or erased.

9.5

Catalog Files

Important files in the <CPMUG> and <PC-BLUE> archives are the CATALOG files. These files, which are stored in ASCII, contain the "-CATALOG.nnn" files from all the volumes of their respective archives. To obtain these composite catalog files, connect to SIMTEL20 via FTP and do this:

```
get pd:<cpmug>cpmug.cat
get pd:<pc-blue.vol000>pcblue.cat
```

A similar file exists for the <SIGM> archive, but it is stored in squeezed form. This file, when unsqueezed, yields SIG.CAT (the catalog). It can be obtained using the FTP command:

```
get pd:<sigm.vol000>sig.cqt
```

(NOTE: That's "L-and-three-zeros" in "vol000")

Chapter 10

Other Repositories on SIMTEL20

There are nine repositories on SIMTEL20 at the time of this writing:

ADA	–the Ada Software Repository
CPM	–for CP/M users
CPMUG	–the CP/M UsersGroup'
MSDOS	–for MSDOS (IBM PC and compatible) users
PC-BLUE	–the PC/BLUE UsersGroup'
SIGM	–the Special Interest Group in CP/M
UNIX	–for UNIX users
ZSYS	–for ZCPR3 and Z System users
MISC	–miscellaneous items, such as TOPS-20 and VAXVMS

The PD:<CPM> repository contains the latest CP/M offerings, and it is updated frequently. The PD:<CPMUG>, PD:<SIGM> and PD:<PC-BLUE> repositories contain software distributed by the CP/M Users Group, the SIG/M Users Group and the PC-Blue Users Group, respectively. This software is available on diskettes from the associated users groups, and the repositories are updated as new volumes are issued.

The PD:<PC-BLUE> repository contains software for the IBM-PC and similar machines. Some of this software runs under CP/M-86, and some runs under PCDOS/MSDOS. The PD:<MSDOS> repository also contains software for the MSDOS and PCDOS operating systems. This repository is locally managed, and therefore is updated more frequently than the PD:<PC-BLUE> repository.

The PD:<UNIX> repository contains a variety of UNIX tools. Those which apply specifically to CP/M are in the directory PD:<UNIX.CPM>.

The PD:<ADA> repository contains Ada software and information related to the Ada effort. Information about this repository is in directory PD:<ADA.GENERAL>.

The PD:<ZSYS> repository contains files of interest to users of ZCPR3 and the Z System associated with ZCPR3.

The PD:<MISC> repository contains files which do not fit into the other repositories. PD:<MISC.TOPS-20> contains programs specific to the TOPS-20 operating system, and PD:<MISC.VAXVMS> contains programs specific to the VAX VMS operating system. PD:<MISC> also contains other subdirectories worth scanning.

10.1 CRCLST Files

Each repository has, in its top-level directory, files called CRCLST files:

pd:<ada>ada.crclst
pd:<cpm>cpm.crclst
pd:<cpmug>cpmug.crclst
pd:<msdos>msdos.crclst
pd:<pc-blue>pc-blue.crclst
pd:<sigm>sigm.crclst
pd:<unix>unix.crclst
pd:<zsys>zsys.crclst
pd:<misc>misc.crclst

These files are text files which contain directory listings of their respective repositories.

10.2 Electronic Mailing Lists

The users of the various repositories can interact with each other on a number of electronic mailing lists. Some lists of particular interest are:

1. ADA-SW - for Ada users (with information on the ADA repository)
2. INFO-CPM - for CP/M users (with information on the CPM, CPMUG, SIGM, and ZSYS repositories)

3. INFO-IBMPC - for IBM PC users (with information on the the PC-BLUE and MSDOS repositories)

4. UNIX-SW - for UNIX users (with information on the UNIX repository)

See the chapter on electronic mailing lists for more details.

Chapter 11

Obtaining Software from the Repositories

The Ada Software Repository and the other repositories on SIMTEL20 can be accessed through three mechanisms:

1. FTP - File Transfer Protocol
2. Archive Server
3. Tape Distribution

This chapter describes how to use these three mechanisms to access the repositories, particularly the Ada Software Repository.

The user community of the repositories on SIMTEL20 can be divided into three classes:

1. Users who employ a host computer that is directly connected to the Defense Data Network.
2. Users who employ a host computer that is connected to a network which in turn interfaces to the DDN through a gateway, but only by electronic mail.
3. Other users.

If you are a class-1 user (direct connection to the DDN), all three methods of accessing the repositories are available to you. FTP is the fastest and most timely; you can employ the Archive Server but are encouraged to use FTP and the tape distribution rather than the Archive Server.

If you are a class-2 user (access to the DDN via a network gateway that passes only electronic mail), only the Archive Server and the tape distribution are available to you. The Archive Server was created specifically for this class of users. For class-3 users, only the tape distribution is available.

11.1 Using FTP

FTP (File Transfer Protocol) is the Defense Data Network InterNet file transfer protocol. It can be used to transfer files efficiently and reliably between any two host computers on the Defense Data Network. Specifically, you can use it to transfer files, with a minimum of effort, from the repositories on SIMTEL20 and other DDN hosts to your local host computer.

FTP is a formalized procedure for moving files among machines on the Defense Data Network (DDN) and other networks that connect with the DDN. The protocol is implemented by a program often called FTP. The different mainframe operating systems implement FTP with variations in command syntax. On some systems, the remote filename must precede the local filename in the command. Other systems reverse this order. Some versions require the whole command to be on a single input line, whereas others allow multiple lines. You'll find all information about a particular FTP implementation in the hard-copy or on-line documentation for that system. If this documentation is not available, consult your system-support personnel for the details of local FTP command syntax.

UNIX users can issue a command like "man ftp" to obtain on-line help. Not all UNIX FTP programs are called "ftp", so you may have to snoop around in the system directories or ask a system wizard for the correct local name to use with the "man" command. ITS users can give the command ":INFO FTP"; "HELP FTP" works on TOPS-20 and some other operating systems.

11.1.1 Generic FTP Syntax

Throughout this section, FTP examples are given in a generic syntax. For the specific syntax of your host's operating-system commands and FTP tools, consult either the on-line documentation provided by your host, or your local system-support personnel.

For the sake of brevity, the domain suffix ".ARPA" will be dropped from further references to SIMTEL20 in this discussion of FTP. The fully-qualified name for SIMTEL20 is "SIMTEL20.ARPA".

11.1.2 Anonymous Login

Certain DDN host computers, including SIMTEL20, can be viewed as "glass houses." Anyone on the DDN can log into them by using the anonymous login convention of FTP, in which you specify "anonymous" as the user name and your host computer's name (or any other string of printing characters) as the password. Note, however, that this anonymous login convention is available *only* through FTP. You can't use the anonymous login convention unless you're already in FTP.

11.1.3 Directory Listings by FTP

To obtain directory listings, connect to SIMTEL20 via FTP and issue any or all of the following commands:

```
get pd:<ada>ada.crclst
get pd:<cpm>cpm.crclst
get pd:<cpmug>cpmug.crclst
get pd:<msdos>msdos.crclst
get pd:<pc-blue>pc-blue.crclst
get pd:<sigm>sigm.crclst
get pd:<unix>unix.crclst
get pd:<zsys>zsys.crclst
get pd:<misc>misc.crclst
```

The crclst files are text files containing directory listings of their respective repositories. See the chapter on TOPS-20 and SIMTEL20 for more details on these repositories.

Many FTP programs support a DIR command that sends directory displays from the remote computer to the user. The generic form of this command for users accessing SIMTEL20 is:

```
DIR device:<directory.subdirectory>
```

See the chapter on TOPS-20 and SIMTEL20 for details on available devices and directories.

11.1.4

Change Working Directory by FTP

SIMTEL20 supports the FTP "change working directory" command (the local syntax may be something like CD or CWD). Ignore the message that prompts you to enter a password. The password is required only if the user is going to PUT files into SIMTEL20 (ie, send files from his local host computer to SIMTEL20). The CD command allows a user to specify a default SIMTEL20 directory to be used for all file retrievals, thereby relieving the user from having to repeatedly type "device:<directory>" as part of each filename. For example, you can use a series of commands like:

```
cd pd:<cpm.goodstuff>
get filename-1
get filename-2
```

instead of:

```
get pd:<cpm.goodstuff>filename-1
get pd:<cpm.goodstuff>filename-2
```

11.1.5

File Transfer by FTP

Use the GET command to obtain files from the remote computer onto your local computer via FTP. Use the PUT command to place files on the remote computer from your local computer. For the purposes of this discussion, only GET will be covered.

The DDN can handle a wide variety of file-transfer modes, and when a more efficient mode is available to you, you can use it to increase the transfer speed. In linking with SIMTEL20 via FTP, for example, users of TOPS-10, TENEX, TOPS-20 or ITS systems can use "image" or "paged" mode for all transfers. UNIX users must employ "ascii" mode for ASCII files, and "tenex" or "type L 8" mode for binary files. MULTICS users can employ "ascii" mode for ASCII files, but binary files require special treatment that is best described by the example provided by Paul Schauble <Schauble@mit-multics.arpa> (see Figure 11-1).

```
ftp simtel20
220 SIMTEL20.ARPA FTP Server Process 5Z(14)-7 at Mon
                10-Sep-84 00:27-MDT
user_ftp: login anonymous
331 ANONYMOUS user ok, send real ident as password.
Password: guest
user_ftp: quote "type l 8" <--(NOTE: That's lowercase "L" 8.)
200 Type L bytesize 8 ok.
user_ftp: get micro:<cpm.zcpr3>alias.hlp alias.hlp
150 Retrieve of MICRO:<CPM.ZCPR3>ALIAS.HLP.1 started.
226 Transfer completed.
Total elapsed time: 35.7 seconds.
4348 bytes transferred in 18.5 seconds (1850 bits/sec).
user_ftp: quit
221 QUIT command received. Goodbye.
```

Figure 11-1. FTP Example

In this dialogue, characters in *italics* are typed by the user. The received files are stored on MULTICS with one 8-bit byte per 9-bit word, and can be transferred to a microcomputer with Kermit or some other protocol.

All aspects of the FTP process for UNIX machines have been automated to a high degree by a program in directory PD:<UNIX.CPM>. With this program, a simple command like "mb modm700.com" can connect to SIMTEL20 and transfer the binary file "modm700.com" from directory PD:<CPM.MODEM7> to a local file also named "modm700.com" with no user intervention. You can run batch command files, containing multiple lines of the form in the above example, in no-hangup background mode in order to transfer whole directories; you need not even remain logged into yourlocal system. For more information, get the file: PD:<UNIX.CPM>AUTOFTP.DOC.

11.2 Archive Server

The Archive Server is a program that receives electronic mail, containing commands such as "SEND format filename," and processes those commands. It allows you to obtain directory displays of, and files from, the repositories on SIMTEL20.

11.2.1 Address of Archive Server

The electronic mail address of the Archive Server is

ARCHIVE-REQUEST@SIMTEL20.ARPA

Subscribers to USENET, and to other UUCP-based networks that are connected to the DDN via electronic mail gateways, can access the Archive Server by employing the following gateway-oriented addresses:

...!ucbvax!simtel20.arpa!archive-request

...!uw-beaver!simtel20.arpa!archive-request

...!decwrl!simtel20.arpa!archive-request

...!lll-crg!simtel20.arpa!archive-request

11.2.2 Message Body

The body of the electronic mail message must contain only lines beginning with the keyword SEND. Case is not significant, and the general syntax of the SEND line is:

SEND verb or

SEND format filename

The "SEND verb" form transmits specific information about Archive Server to the user. The allowed forms of "SEND verb" are:

1. SEND HELP. A brief information file on how to use Archive Server is mailed to the requester.

2. SEND INFO. A detailed description of the repositories on SIMTEL20, the brief information file transmitted by the "SEND HELP" command, pointers to certain key files, and descriptions of various file transfer programs and related utilities are all transmitted to the requester.

3. SEND BOOTSTRAP. A brief quick reference listing of filenames of the key utilities that you'll use to reconstruct compressed or encoded files sent by the techniques used to store certain files in the repositories.

The "SEND format filespec" form transmits either a directory display or a specific file to the requester. Each SEND command can transmit only one directory display or one file—wildcards are not allowed in SEND commands that request file transmissions. If the file to be sent is larger than 55K bytes, it is sent in more than one electronic mail message. There is no guarantee that you'll receive these messages in the order in which they were sent; for this reason, each message is numbered in the subject line so that you'll be able to reassemble the parts in the proper order. During the reconstruction process, you'll have to remove the headers and trailers contained in each message, otherwise they'll prevent you from reconstructing the file in its original form.

Two allowed forms of the "SEND format file" command are:

1. SEND DIR filespec. This form returns a CRC list of the the requested files. This is the only format which allows wildcard filenames (but not wildcard directory names). The list is sent as an ASCII text file.

2. SEND RAW filename. If the file is ASCII, it is sent as-is, regardless of size. This form is the least efficient in terms of network and mail gateway resource utilization. Use this format only if there is no other choice.

The following four forms are used to send files in various text, compressed, and encoded formats. If the file is ASCII and under 25K characters, it is sent as-is (just as if you had requested the RAW form. Binary files are always processed according to the requested format. However, a request for ARC or SQ processing of files with type .ARC, .LBR, or .%Q% is ignored and the original file is either uuencoded or hexified (if possible), according to the requested format. If the file was not sent RAW, at the front of the message you'll find a short preface describing the process actually taken, and a CRC entry describing the original file. The forms of the SEND command are:

1. SEND ARE filename or SEND filename. The original file is made into a uuencoded ARC file.
2. SEND ARH filename. The original file is made into a hexified ARC file if the ARC file is under 64K bytes long. Otherwise, an apology is returned instead of the requested file.
3. SEND SQE filename. The original file is made into a uuencoded SQueezed file.
4. SEND SQH filename. The original file is made into a hexified SQueezed file, provided that the Squeezed file is under 64K bytes long. Otherwise, an apology is returned instead of the requested file.

11.2.3 Archive Server Operation

The ARCHIVE-REQUEST address is serviced by a batch job that reschedules itself one hour after it completes the current pass. That frequency is subject to change.

11.3 Tape Distribution

Tape copies of the files in PD:<ADA*> may be made on 9-track, 1600-bpi tapes in TOPS-20 DUMPER, TOPS-10 INTERCHANGE, and Unix Tar formats. To acquire tapes of the Ada Software Repository, send three tapes, a stamped, self-addressed mailing label, and a short, informal cover letter stating that you want a copy of the Ada Software Repository. Specify the tape format. Personnel at White Sands will make the tape at their convenience, and will mail it back using the enclosed mailing label and stamps. There is no charge for this service.

Use the following address to send the tapes. White Sands cannot accept cash, checks, money orders or purchase orders. Send sufficient return postage in stamps.

Commander
USA White Sands Missile Range
STEWS-IM-CM-S (Bldg. 362, Frank Wancho)
White Sands Missile Range, New Mexico 88002-5072

The other repositories on SIMTEL20 may also be distributed via tape. Contact White Sands for details.

SECTION III: THE ADA SOFTWARE REPOSITORY

— Outline —

Notes

Chapter 12

History and Statement of Operation of the ASR

The Ada Software Repository (ASR) was founded in November, 1984, by Richard Conn with the encouragement and support of Frank Wancho, manager of SIMTEL20. The ASR resides on SIMTEL20, a DEC-20 mainframe computer running the TOPS-20 operating system. SIMTEL20 is located at the White Sands Missile Range in New Mexico and can be accessed through the Defense Data Network (DDN).

The Ada Software Repository is a volunteer effort. The ASR occupies more than 38 Mbytes of disk space, sharing space with other repositories. The disk drive holding these repositories is funded by the Logistics System Support Activity (LSSA), an Army Materiel Command (AMC, formerly DARCOM) organization. LSSA provided funds for a 512 Mbyte disk drive to support the UNIX/C repository for the AMC community. The ASR, along with six other software repositories, occupies some additional space on this disk drive

SIMTEL20 is located at, owned by, and operated by, the Computer Systems Directorate at White Sands Missile Range (WSMR), an Installation/Field Operating Activity (I/FOA) under the Test and Evaluation Command (TECOM). TECOM, located at Aberdeen Proving Ground in Maryland, is a major subordinate command under AMC, while AMC is a major command under the Department of the Army. The primary purposes of SIMTEL20 are to run software simulations used at White Sands and to provide general computing services to military and contractor personnel working on DoD projects in general.

Chapter 13

Online Documentation System

The Ada Software Repository is a fantastic resource, but it would have very limited value without adequate documentation. The purpose of the ASR is to provide a base of reusable Ada software components, tools, and information to all who need them; therefore, the content of the ASR must be documented in a fashion that allows its users to determine what is in the ASR and whether a particular item is of value to them. The online documentation system of the ASR was specially designed to allow users to make these determinations easily, and consists of two parts: A database file that a user can copy to his own host computer, together with a set of programs for accessing the database (and the documentation relating to them); A set of software tools and their documentation, all resident on SIMTEL20, that is used to create and update the database and to support configuration management of the ASR.

13.1 Documentation for the ASR User

Documentation available to the ASR user includes:

1. The software and database stored in the directory PD:<ADA.ONLINE-DOC> in the ASR;
2. The ADA-SW electronic mailing list, over which the users of the ASR communicate with each other, and the archives for this mailing list, which are stored in the directory named PS:<ARCHIVES.ADA> on SIMTEL20; and
3. The ASR newsletters, which are available in the ASR subdirectory named PD:<ADA.NEWS> (these are also available in hardcopy form for a

subscription fee from Echelon Inc, Los Altos, CA), the book entitled *The Master Index to the Ada Software Repository*, which is a loose-leaf book that describes all items of software and documentation in the ASR, and this book.

The database file (item 1, above) is the primary reference for all Ada software in the repository and is periodically updated. To make it easier for you to access it quickly and without tying up network resources, you can transfer the database file to your own local host, together with the associated database programs (which are written in Ada) that will allow you to query the database interactively. These programs come with their own documentation which describes how to run them and how to customize them for your local host. As the ASR grows and changes, you'll periodically need to replace your copy of the database with the latest version.

The ADA-SW electronic mailing list is used to announce new releases of software to the ASR, to discuss bugs, and to discuss any items of interest to the ASR community. For more details, refer to the sections of this book on mailing lists in general, and the ADA-SW electronic mailing list in particular.

The ASR newsletters are published once a month by Echelon Inc (Los Altos, CA). They are five or more pages in size and contain announcements of new software released in the ASR; all software-release announcements posted to ADA-SW are also placed in the newsletters. In addition, they contain information on software bugs (which was also posted to ADA-SW) and other items of interest to users of the Ada Software Repository. The newsletters are available in machine-readable form in the ASR subdirectory PD:<ADA.NEW> and in hardcopy form from Echelon. For details on the hardcopy subscription, contact Echelon Inc directly, at 885 N San Antonio Rd, Los Altos, CA 94022, (415) 948-3820.

The Master Index to the Ada Software Repository is a loose-leaf book that contains details on each software item and each information file in the ASR. Each software item is described by an abstract, information on the host compiler, host operating system, and target environment, and a listing of all associated files and their locations in the ASR. Each information file is described by an abstract and a listing of all associated files. Contact Echelon for details on how to purchase the *Master Index*.

13.2 Documentation Support on SIMTEL20

The online and hardcopy documentation available to the ASR user is supported by a collection of programs, command files, and data files resident on SIMTEL20. These programs and command files create directory displays, place text files and directory displays into the database file in the proper order, index the ASR and track its growth, build certain information files (such as the Welcome Message) which are available to the ASR user, and form the heart of the configuration management system for the ASR.

Each item of software submitted to the ASR must be accompanied by a *Prologue File*. This file identifies the software, names its author and how to contact him, provides information about the compiler and operating system on which the software was developed, contains an abstract of the software, and contains a release notice of the software. All software in the ASR is in the public domain and must have an associated Prologue File. The Prologue Files are stored in the ASR along with their software; the SIMTEL20 online documentation system contains various files that are derived from each Prologue File and are used by the system software to create the ASR database and other documentation files. Full details of the online documentation on SIMTEL20 are not to be released at this time.

Chapter 14

Master Index to the ASR

The Master Index to the Ada Software Repository is a loose-leaf book which contains details on the software and information in the ASR. Each item of software is described by an abstract, information on the host compiler and operating system and target environment, and a listing of all associated files and their locations in the ASR. Each item of information is described by an abstract and a listing of all associated files.

The Master Index breaks down the ASR into the following major categories, each presented as separate chapters:

- ASR-Specific Information and Programs
- Artificial Intelligence
- Benchmarks
- Communications
- Reusable Software Components
- Data Base Management
- Documentation
- Graphics
- Project Management
- Ada Software Development Tools
- Other Tools
- the WIS Ada Tool Set

Selected items of information from the ASR are included in the Master Index. These items include the Welcome Message, which gives an extensive introduction to the Ada Software Repository (its operation and use) and the Defense Data Network (with emphasis on the use of FTP to transfer files from the archives on SIMTEL20).

Appendices include (1) a Snapshot of the ASR (ADA.SNP), which names each directory of the ASR and gives the total size of its contents in terms of bytes and lines of code; (2) a listing of all files in each directory of the ASR with file sizes and CRC data (ADA.CRCLST); and (3) a listing of all files in each directory of the ASR with file sizes, line counts, and PAGER hashes (ADA.RPT).

As the ASR grows, updates to the Master Index will be issued. The loose-leaf format of the Master Index was selected to make the update process easier and to allow users to assemble the Master Index and the ASR Newsletters conveniently into loose-leaf binders.

Chapter 15

ASR Newsletters and Electronic Mailing List

15.1

ASR Newsletters

The Ada Software Repository (ASR) newsletter is published monthly by Echelon, Inc. Users of the ASR may freely transfer copies of the newsletter from PD:<ADA.NEWS> via FTP (the newsletters are in the files matching ASR*.DOC). A hardcopy mailing of the newsletter is also available; for current prices, and to place orders, contact:

Echelon, Inc.
885 N. San Antonio Road
Los Altos, CA 94022
415/948-3820

The tables of contents for several ASR newsletters are presented in Figures 15-1 to 15-7.

ASR Newsletter, Issue 1, April 1986

I. ADA SOFTWARE REPOSITORY STATEMENT OF OPERATION
II. GENERAL INFORMATION
- A. How to Find Things
- B. Electronic Mailing List
- C. Tape Distribution

III. NEWS ITEMS CONCERNING THE ADA SOFTWARE REPOSITORY
- A. This Newsletter
- B. New Documents from Echelon
- C. WIS/NOSC Ada Tools Documents
- D. Talks Scheduled
- E. Tape Distribution Problems and Solutions

IV. NEW SUBMISSIONS IN MARCH
V. HIGHLIGHTS OF SELECTED SUBMISSIONS

Figure 15-1. ASR Newsletter Contents, Issue 1

ASR Newsletter, Issue 2, May 1986

I. ADA TECHNOLOGY - SOME INSIGHTS
- A. Experience in Ada Applications
- B. Bugs in Ada (and other) Compilers
- C. Judging Compilation/Linking Time for Ada Programs
- D. Is Ada a Hodgepodge Formed by Committee?
- E. More on the Complexity of Ada
- F. Weakness in Ada

II. GENERAL INFORMATION
- A. Access to the Ada Information Public Account
- B. Ada Information Clearinghouse Newsletter
- C. Validated Ada Computer for the IBM PC/AT

III. NEWS ITEMS CONCERNING THE ADA SOFTWARE REPOSITORY
- A. Data Dictionary Problem Resolved
- B. Rehosting Data Invited
- C. Hardcopy Documentation from Echelon
- D. Talks on the Ada Software Repository
- E. Access to the ASR from Europe
- F. Pending Termination of the ADA20 Accounts
- G. More on Alternate Access to the ASR

IV. NEW SUBMISSIONS IN APRIL

V. HIGHLIGHTS OF SELECTED SUBMISSIONS

Figure 15–2. ASR Newsletter Contents, Issue 2

ASR Newsletter, Issue 3, June 1986

I. THE ADA SOFTWARE REPOSITORY
  A. Who is Using the ASR?
  B. The Magnitude of the ASR
II. GENERAL INFORMATION
  A. Some Feedback on the Usage of the Army's ALS
  B. Standardization at AFIT
  C. Acquiring DDN Users Guides
III. NEWS ITEMS CONCERNING THE ADA SOFTWARE REPOSITORY
  A. Capacity Data
  B. Third Snapshot of the ASR
  C. Hardcopy Documentation from Echelon
  D. Talks on the ASR
  E. Access to the ASR from Europe
  F. Air Force Ada Course and the ASR
IV. NEW SUBMISSIONS IN MAY
V. HIGHLIGHTS OF SELECTED SUBMISSIONS

Figure 15–3. ASR Newsletter Contents, Issue 3

ASR Newsletter, Issue 4, July 1986

I. NEW RELEASES
II. GENERAL INFORMATION
  A. APSE Trends
  B. From Grady Booch: Reusable Software Components Book
III. NEWS ITEMS CONCERNING THE ADA SOFTWARE REPOSITORY
  A. Top 20
  B. Byte and Line Counts in the ASR
  C. PD:<ADA.NEWS>
IV. NEW SUBMISSIONS IN JUNE

Figure 15–4. ASR Newsletter Contents, Issue 4

ASR Newsletter, Issue 5, August 1986

I. OF PARTICULAR INTEREST ...
  A. Master Index to the Ada Software Repository
  B. Ada EXPO '86
II. GENERAL INFORMATION
  A. Ada 1988
  B. Ada Information Clearinghouse Bulletin Board
  C. An Interesting Topic: the Cray 3
  D. The DDN as a Resource: the List of Lists
  E. The JALCF Newsletter
III. NEWS ITEMS CONCERNING THE ADA SOFTWARE REPOSITORY
  A. Export Controls
  B. New Format for Online and Hardcopy Documentation
  C. NOSC-TOOLS Directory Dropped
  D. Growth of the Ada Software Repository
  E. Tape Distribution
IV. NEW SUBMISSIONS IN JULY

Figure 15–5. ASR Newsletter Contents, Issue 5

ASR Newsletter, Issue 6, September 1986

I. DOCUMENTATION ON THE ADA SOFTWARE REPOSITORY
  A. Introduction
  B. Master Index to the Ada Software Repository
  C. The Repository User's Handbook
  D. Ada Software Repository Newsletters
  E. AHELP and Online Documentation
II. NEWS ITEMS CONCERNING THE ADA SOFTWARE REPOSITORY
  A. Archive Server
  B. Caveat Emptor
  C. I Wish to Thank ...

Figure 15–6. ASR Newsletter Contents, Issue 6

ASR Newsletter, Issue 7, October 1986

I. ARCHIVE SERVER
- A. Introduction
- B. Address of the Archive Server
- C. Message Body
- D. Archive Server Operation

II. INFORMATION OF GENERAL INTEREST
- A. Current Air Force, Army, and Navy Policy Concerning Ada
- B. Accounts Available on SIMTEL20
- C. Ada Software Repository Evolution and Control Committee
- D. Talks Scheduled on the Ada Software Repository

III. NEW FILES IN THE ADA SOFTWARE REPOSITORY

Figure 15–7. ASR Newsletter Contents, Issue 7

15.2

Electronic Mailing List for ASR Users

An electronic mailing list exists for those who are interested in accessing and contributing software to the Ada Repository on SIMTEL20. To subscribe to this mailing list, send a request via electronic mail to:

ADA-SW-REQUEST@SIMTEL20

After you have been logged into the repository's mailing list, you will receive a welcome message which provides introductory information on how to access the repository.

The mailing list serves two purposes: to help exchange information between the repository users and to mail repository submissions to the maintainer of the Ada Software Repository for inclusion in the archives.

PS:<ARCHIVES.ADA-SW>ADA-SW-ARCHIV.TXT contains all recent messages passed over the ADA-SW mailing list. New users on the list are invited to get a copy of this file and scan it for background; older users may use it for reference. In either case, *be warned*, this is a BIG file! PS:<ARCHIVES.ADA-SW>ADA-SW.ARCHIVE.ymmdd contains older messages by year/month.

Chapter 16

ASR Control Committee

We now take a slight diversion from the normal "handbook" flavor of this book to discuss a very important subject with respect to the Ada Software Repository: configuration control and quality assurance. Note that this chapter addresses the "concepts of operation" for the ASR. In some cases, not all principles discussed are in effect yet.

The Ada Software Repository Control Committee (ASR-CC) is a restricted electronic mailing list on the DDN and is composed of individuals who are actively involved in promoting the Ada Software Repository. The group was formed in October, 1986, by Richard Conn with the intent to turn the ASR from a one-man operation into a committee operation.

Specific items of interest to the ASR-CC include:

1. Maintenance of the software in the ASR;
2. Configuration management of the ASR;
3. Quality assurance of the software in the ASR.

The mechanisms employed in the operation of the ASR may be of interest to you, particularly, if you are interested in setting up a local software repository, perhaps based on the software in the ASR or other repositories on the DDN. This chapter should provide some insight into the issues to be addressed in the operation of such a repository.

16.1 Software Maintenance

The maintenance of the software in the ASR is perhaps the most difficult subject to address. Maintenance requires resources, primarily manpower, to process Software Performance Reports (SPRs) submitted by users of ASR software on problems they have encountered in its use. One goal of the ASR-CC is to establish formal software maintenance procedures to assure the timely resolution of the reported problems.

One approach to formal software maintenance is:

1. A user encounters a problem with an item of software and fills out an SPR on the problem.
2. A *Change Control Authority* (the ASR-CC or a panel of the ASR-CC) receives the SPR (preferably by electronic mail), reviews it, and assigns to it a priority based on the severity of the problem. The submitter is notified (preferably by electronic mail) that his SPR has been received and initially processed.
3. An *SPR Review Authority* (the ASR-CC or a panel of the ASR-CC) reviews the SPR in order of priority to determine the nature of the problem and attempt an initial resolution of the class of the problem. Classes of problems are:

   a. *Corrective*, in which a correction for the problem already exists,

   b. *Adaptive*, in which the problem can be circumvented without the need to modify the software, and

   c. *Perfective*, in which software maintenance must be performed to correct the problem.
4. If the class of the problem is corrective or adaptive, then the person who submitted the SPR is advised of the correction. If the problem is adaptive, a comment file (CMM) may also be created and stored in the ASR in order to explain to future users of the software the nature of the problem and how it can be circumvented.
5. If the class of the problem is perfective, then the Review Authority estimates the resources required to correct the problem and schedules the work. The SPR is translated into a *Software Change Request* (SCR), which records a more detailed description of the problem and all relevant information uncovered during the

review process. In the case of the ASR, the problem is forwarded to the originator of the software; however, if the originator can not address the problem, then the ASR-CC must call upon its own resources to do so. In any case, the submitter should be kept advised (preferably via electronic mail) of the status of his SPR.

Once the problem has been corrected, the new software is passed through the Configuration Management system into the Ada Software Repository. Comment files (CMM) are generated which document the problem, and these comment files are placed into the ASR. There is no *Unit Development Folder* (UDF) on an item of software in the ASR per se, but the files for a software item, including the comment files, make up the essence of a UDF.

16.1.1 Problem Correction

As a result of the formalized problem report and evaluation procedure outlined above, similar (related) errors may be scheduled for correction concurrently, thereby eliminating redundant maintenance tasks. It is up to the person or organization making the correction to adopt and follow procedures which are satisfactory to them.

One approach to problem correction is to anticipate the need for it and to create a *Unit Development Folder* (UDF) from the very start in order to maintain each software item (unit) and track its corrections. A UDF typically contains the following items:

1. A history of the changes made to the unit;
2. Source code of the current version of the unit;
3. Design documents on the unit, including documents from design reviews and *Program Design Language* (PDL) files which express the design of the unit in a very readable form;
4. Test plans and test procedures, including test cases for the unit; and
5. Information to aid in tracking the unit in the configuration management system.

The maintenance task parallels the design, code, and test steps for new software development. A systematic technique, such as the use of SPRs and SCRs as outlined above, should be employed to report and correct problems. The person or organization controlling the maintenance of the software should consider the following topics:

1. Acceptance of tested software;
2. Release criteria for the software;
3. Configuration management of the software;
4. Coordination of personnel; and
5. Record keeping on the maintenance activity.

In accepting tested software, checks should be made to verify that the documentation is complete and up to date, that all test cases have been run successfully, and that the software has been properly placed under configuration management. The criteria for the release of the software should be that all of these requirements have been met.

The configuration management of the software usually involves the assignment of a new *revision number* or *version number* to the software and the establishment of a new baseline of the software. A distinction is made here between a revision and a version of software.

A *revision* is a new release of software which is intended to correct one or more classes of errors encountered after the original software was released. The revision may also add simple functional changes, improve performance, or implement an adaptation of the software to a new environment. When critical software errors are encountered ("critical" is determined by the Software Review Authority in many cases), the maintenance organization may release a temporary fix to the software to enable the user to circumvent the problem until a revision is issued; each revision should incorporate all pending temporary fixes. A revision is compatible with earlier revisions, implying that the earlier test cases may also be applied to test this revision.

On the other hand, a *version* generally incorporates all revisions made to date and may be used to introduce major enhancements that extend the scope of the original software. New, and sometimes radically different, functions may be incorporated into a new version of software, and compatibility with previous versions of the software may not be possible. The documentation released with the new version should outline the functional differences and their impact on the user.

Continuing with the five maintenance tasks itemized above, another task is that of coordinating personnel. Members of the maintenance team of the ASR-CC should have a working knowledge of all software configurations in the ASR so that decisions can be made as to how to address the maintenance issue on a case-by-case basis. If the submitters are willing to perform the maintenance, then they should be given the first opportunity. If the submitters are not responsive or are not willing to maintain their software, then the ASR maintenance team should determine how the software will be supported and implement a mechanism for this. Within a typical maintenance organization, there is no one correct approach. The number of people in the organization, the amount of software to be maintained, and the nature of the software (whether it is public domain, a commercial product, or for internal use) are factors which determine how the maintenance of the software will be done. Likewise, these factors will also help determine what kinds of records will be kept on the software.

16.2 Configuration Management

The configuration of a software unit consists of:

1. The software itself in machine-readable form;
2. Source listings of the software;
3. Documentation on the software, including design documents, documents Unit Development Folders, maintenance manuals, user's manuals, prologue files (specifically in the case of the ASR software), test documentation, planning documentation, and software requirements specifications; and

4. Test data, test programs, and expected results for the software.

In software configuration management, the configuration of the software at a particular instant in time is recorded and formally managed. Software configuration management consists of four basic tasks:

1. Establishment of documentation standards and a document identification scheme;
2. Change control, which is the evaluation and recording of all changes to the software configuration;
3. Accurate tracking and controlled access to documents pertaining to the software; and
4. A continuous audit of the software configuration.

The responsibility of configuration management generally lies outside of the developers and is ideally suited to coordination by a software librarian. Software configuration management is a key function of the Ada Software Repository, and the tasks of the software configuration management process, as implemented for the ASR, are described throughout the section of this book on the ASR and in a companion volume, *The Master Index to the Ada Software Repository.*

16.3 Quality Assurance

While one of the tasks of software configuration management is to establish documentation and change control standards for the software, the enforcement of those standards is assigned to quality assurance. Some organizations support a *Software Quality Assurance* (SQA) suborganization. The role of SQA is to check on development and maintenance suborganizations in order to ensure that the documentation, software development, and software maintenance standards are being followed. In the case of the ASR, the ASR-CC performs the quality assurance function.

Chapter 17

Directories in the Ada Software Repository

The following is a summary of the directories in the Ada Software Repository (ASR) on the SIMTEL20 host computer. The ASR is located on the disk structure named PD: (for Public Domain) under the top-level directory named PD:<ADA>. The ASR directory structure is a two-level tree, and the root is ADA. All subdirectories are direct descendents of the ADA root, and names of subdirectories take the form of PD:<ADA.XXX>, where XXX is a subdirectory name, like PD:<ADA.BENCHMARKS>.

17.1 Ada Software Repository Support

Directory: PD:<ADA>

This is the top-level directory. The names of the subdirectories (*.DIRECTORY) can be seen here. The listing of all files in all subdirectories (ADA.CRCLST) and the listing of all files in the ASR ordered by frequency of access (FILEUSE.DOC) are stored herein.

Directory: PD:<ADA.NEWS>

The NEWS subdirectory contains the Ada Software Repository (ASR) Newsletters. They are numbered sequentially, starting at 001, with file names like ASRnnn.DOC. Ada Information Clearinghouse newsletters, named AIC*.DOC, and snapshots of the Ada Software Repository, named SNAP*.DOC, are also contained herein. The ASR snapshots list the subdirectory names and sizes, allowing the user to review the growth and status of the Ada Software Repository.

Directory: PD:<ADA.ONLINE-DOC>

The ONLINE-DOC subdirectory contains supporting files for the on-line documentation system of the Ada Software Repository. The database file that describes all entries in the Ada Software Repository as well as the Ada programs used to access this file interactively, are contained herein.

Directory: PD:<ADA.PAGER>

The PAGER subdirectory contains tools which create and manipulate paged files. All *.SRC files are paged files, which are files composed of several smaller files separated by special prefix lines. The PAGER tool is written in Ada and is needed to extract component files from the *.SRC files if similar tools do not already exist on the user's computer system.

Directory: PD:<ADA.STARTER-KIT>

The STARTER-KIT subdirectory contains pointers to tools that are useful in accessing the software in the repository. It points to the PAGER tool, which is used to assemble and disassemble SRC (paged) files, and to the online documentation facility tools.

17.2 Artificial Intelligence

Directory: PD:<ADA.AI>

The AI subdirectory contains programs relating to the fields of artificial intelligence, such as expert systems, pattern recognition, and heuristic analysis.

The source code and documentation, which amount to more than 500k bytes, include a simple expert system and a reusable software components package that implements several LISP functions in Ada.

17.3 Benchmarks

Directory: PD:<ADA.BENCHMARKS>

The BENCHMARKS subdirectory contains various Ada compiler benchmarks. An attempt has been made to see that entries in this subdirectory do not duplicate entries in the <BENCHMARK> directory on USC-ECLB. Benchmarks submitted in conjunction with the WIS/NOSC tools are located in the Ada Repository BENCHMARKS subdirectory.

17.4 Common APSE Interface Set

Directory: PD:<ADA.CAIS>

The CAIS subdirectory contains software associated with the Common APSE Interface Set (CAIS). The CAIS is defined in MIL-STD-CAIS.

Directory: PD:<ADA.CAIS-TOOLS>

The CAIS-TOOLS subdirectory contains tools which are compatible with, and modified or implemented to run under, the CAIS presented in the directory PD:<ADA.CAIS>. These tools have been modified or implemented by Mitre Corporation and internally funded by Mitre. The PD:<ADA.CAIS> and PD:<ADA.CAIS-TOOLS> subdirectories contain over 3M bytes of source code and documentation.

17.5 Communications

Directory: PD:<ADA.DDN>

The DDN subdirectory contains tools and components related to the Defense Data Network, including its file transfer, mail, and communications facilities. Implementations of the TCP/IP communications protocol, the FTP file transfer tool, and the SMTP mail handling protocol are included, amounting to over 2M bytes of source code and documentation.

Directory: PD:<ADA.MESSAGE-HANDLING>

The MESSAGE-HANDLING subdirectory contains tools for use in message-handling facilities and message transfer. The Generic Message Handling Facility (GMHF) and the UNITREP Software Model are included, amounting to over 1M bytes of source code and documentation.

17.6 Reusable Software Components

Directory: PD:<ADA.COMPONENTS>

The COMPONENTS subdirectory contains a variety of reusable software components and is the most popular subdirectory in the Ada Software Repository. Containing over 2M bytes of source code and documentation, the COMPONENTS subdirectory contains general-purpose procedures, packages, and generics. Examples include: an Ada statement parser and two parsing-component libraries, TERMCAP routines, generic linked-list packages, dynamic string-manipulation packages, Ada statement counters, queue-manipulation components, a generic Quicksort routine, other sort routines, stack–manipulation routines, and additional I/O support routines. Most of the entries are packages or generic packages.

Directory: PD:<ADA.MATH>

The MATH subdirectory contains packages of math routines written in Ada. Routines for trig functions, exponential functions, matrix manipulation, bit manipulation, set manipulation, logical functions, 36-bit machine arithmetic, and others are contained here.

17.7

Database Management

Directory: PD:<ADA.ADA-SQL>

The ADA-SQL subdirectory contains files associated with the development of a standard Ada DBMS interface (Ada/SQL) based on the dpANS Database Language SQL. It is anticipated that SQL will be adopted as the Air Force standard Relational database query language.

Included in more than 1M bytes of source code and documentation in ADA-SQL are the RAPPORT and DAMES database management system (DBMS) interfaces. These were developed to define an Ada DBMS interface and are provided for information purposes only.

Directory: PD:<ADA.DBMS>

The DBMS subdirectory contains Ada software components and programs directly related to database management functions. An implementation of the Mobile Information Management System is contained herein.

17.8

Documentation

Directory: PD:<ADA.ANSI-LRM>

The ANSI-LRM subdirectory contains a machine-readable copy of the ANSI Version of the Ada Language Reference Manual (LRM). The files were obtained from the directory <ADA- LSN> on ECLB, and the file FTPFILES.SUB shows the FTP process used to copy the files and rename some of them. Chapters 1-14 and Appendices A-F are included as CHAPxx.DOC (like, CHAP01.DOC or CHAPA.DOC). Error files are also included as CHAPxx.ERR. The Foreword (FOREWORD.DOC, FOREWORD.ERR), Postscript (POSTSCRPT.DOC, POSTSCRPT.ERR), and Table of Contents (TOC.DOC) are included. INDEX.DOC contains the index.

Directory: PD:<ADA.EDUCATION>

The EDUCATION subdirectory contains sample Ada programs, tutorials, and online courseware. Included are notes on common Ada programming errors, Ada and FORTRAN interfacing, a glossary of Ada terms, and reviews of Ada text books.

Directory: PD:<ADA.GENERAL>

The GENERAL subdirectory is the General Information subdirectory. Notes, comments, usage information, and other data are stored here. Included are copyright information, information and tutorials on using the File Transfer Protocol (FTP), general information on the Kermit file transfer protocol, and general information for users of the Ada Software Repository.

Directory: PD:<ADA.POINTERS>

The POINTERS subdirectory contains information on other sources of software and information (such as the ADA20 resources). This data pertains to both on- and off-net resources. Included are information on how to access the data files on ADA20, how to obtain copies of the Ada Compiler Validation Capability Test Suite, a list of planned Ada implementations, key points of contact in the Ada community (including names, addresses, and phone numbers of personnel in the Ada Joint Program Office), a list of currently validated Ada compilers, and data on a variety of Ada- oriented programs.

Directory: PD:<ADA.WIS-ADA-TOOLS>

The WIS-ADA-TOOLS subdirectory contains information about the software tools submitted by the Naval Oceans Systems Center (NOSC). An abstract of the tools is included.

These tools were paid for by WIS (WWMCCS Information Systems).

17.9

Graphics

Directory: PD:<ADA.GKS>

The GKS subdirectory contains routines associated with a Graphical Kernel System. GKS includes a device-independent software package which implements the draft GKS binding to ANSI Ada for GKS levels Ma, Oa, 1a, 2a, Mb, Ob, 1B, Mc, and 1c.

17.10

Project Management

Directory: PD:<ADA.MANAGEMENT-TOOLS>

The MANAGEMENT-TOOLS subdirectory contains tools for use in managing an Ada software development project. Status–tracking and manpower-estimation tools are included. Some of these tools may be applied to any software development project. The MANAGEMENT-TOOLS subdirectory includes tools for:

- project cost estimation
- project status tracking
- project manpower estimation
- project requirements tracking

17.11

Ada Software Development Tools

The subdirectories which fall into this category contain more than 9.5M bytes of source code and documentation.

Directory: PD:<ADA.COMPILATION-ORDER>

The COMPILATION-ORDER subdirectory contains software that deals with the analysis of groups of Ada programs to determine the proper compilation order. Other information pertaining to the interrelationship of software segments of a system may be obtained as well.

Directory: PD:<ADA.CROSS-REFERENCE>

The CROSS-REFERENCE subdirectory contains tools that generate cross-reference listings of Ada programs.

Directory: PD:<ADA.DEBUGGER>

The DEBUGGER subdirectory contains Ada source-level debuggers. A Symbolic Debugger is included.

Directory: PD:<ADA.FORMGEN>

The FORMGEN subdirectory contains tools for the generation of forms for use by Ada programs. The forms generator will display and accept input into a form (in a screen-oriented fashion via the virtual terminal) in such a way that this mechanism is transparent to the Ada program using it. Instead, the program simply reads fields from the form via procedure interfaces.

Directory: PD:<ADA.MENU>

The MENU subdirectory contains software used in the generation of menus. Applications programs may use these menu generators as front-ends.

Directory: PD:<ADA.METRICS>

The METRICS subdirectory contains tools used to perform metrics analysis of Ada software. Tools for path analysis, performance analysis, and other metrics reports are included. Specific tools include:

* an automatic path analyzer which traces paths executed in an Ada program and records the execution frequency

* Halstead and McCabe complexity measures report generators

* a performance analyzer which measures system timing of Ada program units

* a metric analysis tool that measures program timing loop execution counts, state of control variables at decision points, and the maximum, minimum, and average values of selected variables.

Directory: PD:<ADA.TOOLS>

The TOOLS subdirectory contains miscellaneous tools. Sources to various tools which do not fit into the categories of the other subdirectories are placed here.

Included are tools which:

* count the number of Ada statements in bodies of code

* compute checksums on text files

Directory: PD:<ADA.PDL>

The PDL subdirectory contains software associated with Ada Program Design Languages and tools to support the Ada program designer. Such tools include tools for data–dictionary manipulation and design analysis. There may be some overlap between this directory and software which may fall into the PDL category that is scattered among the other subdirectories.

Directory: PD:<ADA.PRETTY-PRINTERS>

The PRETTY-PRINTERS subdirectory contains pretty printers for Ada source programs. The pretty printers reformat the Ada source programs in order to outline the structure of the programs and provide other useful information for the programmer.

Directory: PD:<ADA.STUBBER>

The STUBBER subdirectory contains Ada program body stubber tools. They analyze the definition of an Ada software design and generate software bodies as stubs to be filled in later during development.

Directory: PD:<ADA.STYLE>

The STYLE subdirectory contains Ada style checking tools. They analyze Ada source code and report on various aspects of the programming style, such as consistent indentation and use of long variable names.

Directory: PD:<ADA.VIRTERM>

The VIRTERM subdirectory contains components for a virtual terminal package, which performs screen-oriented functions by reading terminal characteristics from a UNIX–like TERMCAP data base. The application program can call routines in these packages and not be concerned with the type of terminal being addressed.

17.12

Other Tools

Directory: PD:<ADA.EDITORS>

The EDITORS subdirectory contains the source code and documentation on some text editors written in Ada.

Directory: PD:<ADA.EXTERNAL-TOOLS>

The EXTERNAL-TOOLS subdirectory contains several miscellaneous tools which are helpful in developing Ada code but are not written in Ada and don't pertain to specific environments. For example, an Ada language development interface for the EMACS editor can be found here.

Directory: PD:<ADA.SIMULATION>

The SIMULATION subdirectory contains programs and tools associated with performing simulations, such as queuing simulations.

Directory: PD:<ADA.SPELLER>

The SPELLER subdirectory contains spelling checkers written in Ada. Dictionaries are also included here.

Chapter 18

Lessons Learned about Ada Software Transportability

One of the primary objectives in the creation of the Ada programming language was transportability of Ada software between different host computers and environments without modification. The DDN provides an effective medium for the transfer of files between different host computers, and the Ada Software Repository, located on a DDN host computer, provides a bridge between the two DoD cornerstones of Ada and the DDN. Users of the Ada Software Repository are gaining much experience in the transporting of Ada software into various environments, and this chapter outlines some of the lessons learned from these experiences.

18.1 Problems in Transporting Ada Code

The ASR has shown innumerable times that Ada source code can be transported from one Ada compiler and computing environment to another with ease. There is a caveat, however. The code must have been designed with transportability in mind. In spite of the Ada compiler validation procedure, Ada compilers still exhibit differences that hinder transportability.

One such difference lies in the way of implementing the standard Ada I/O package TEXT_IO. For instance, some compilers cause the GET routine for characters to return each character to the calling program immediately, as it is entered, without first filling an internal buffer, whereas other compilers cause the GET routine not to return any characters to the calling program until the input buffer is filled (that is, the user has typed a full line of text followed by a carriage return). This problem prevents the creation of transportable software with a more user-friendly interface (specifically, the creation of software that responds immediately to a single keypress) and forces all transportable software to be written using the GET_LINE routine rather than the GET routine.

Another difference is that the various Ada compiler implementations may raise different types of exception in response to the same error condition. There are many other differences in the details of compiler implementation that can hinder transportability of the code.

There have been many discussions of such discoveries via the INFO-ADA electronic mailing list and, as a result, the people maintaining the validation test suite are constantly pulling such reports off the network and adding more tests to the test suite. The overall effect is a tighter, more complete test suite that will continue to evolve and reduce the differences between the various Ada compilers.

18.2 Generics

Generics have proven to be invaluable in the creation of transportable Ada software. Ever since the formation of the ASR, the popularity of the various software items in the ASR has been tracked by the frequency of access to the files, and you'll usually find five or more reusable generic software components among the ten most popular software items. More and more reusable software components in the ASR are generic.

18.3 Input/Output

Input and output by Ada programs has been the single biggest stumbling block in the transportability of software from the ASR. The Ada package capability, however, provides a mechanism to reduce I/O-related transportability problems significantly. The answer is to place all input/output routines into a single, clearly identified input/output package. Even if you make use of TEXT_IO, hide the TEXT_IO interface by having this Input/Output package make the calls to TEXT_IO while the rest of the software uses the routines in the Input/Output package.

SECTION IV: OTHER RESOURCES ON THE DDN

— Outline —

Notes

Chapter 19

The Network Information Center (NIC)

The DDN Network Information Center (NIC) provides support to users of the Defense Data Network. The NIC answers queries from users (via telephone, electronic mail, and US mail) and maintains a number of public directories on the NIC host computer. The NIC is located at SRI International in Menlo Park, California, and is funded by the Defense Data Network Defense Communications System (DDN DCS). Points of contact for the NIC are given in Figure 19-1.

The NIC provides a wealth of information to DDN users, in several forms:

1. Hardcopy publications;
2. Online databases of DDN users;
3. Online databases of DDN host computers;
4. Online documentation on the technical aspects of the operation of the DDN;
5. An online newsletter.

19.1 Accessing the NIC from the DDN

All DDN users have the ability to access the Network Information Center directly. To become interactively connected to the NIC from a DDN host computer, just issue the command:

TELNET SRI-NIC or TELNET NIC

If your local node is a TAC, issue the command:

@NIC

Address and Telephone for the NIC

DDN Network Information Center
SRI International, Room EJ291
333 Ravenswood Avenue
Menlo Park, CA 94025
800-235-3155 or (International) +1 415 859-3695

NIC Electronic Mail Addresses

NIC@SRI-NIC.ARPA
General user assistance and document requests
REGISTRAR@SRI-NIC.ARPA
User registration and WHOIS updates
HOSTMASTER@SRI-NIC.ARPA
Host name and domain changes
ACTION@SRI-NIC.ARPA
SRI-NIC computer operations
SUGGESTIONS@SRI-NIC.ARPA
Comments on NIC services and publications
FEINLER@SRI-NIC.ARPA
Manager of the NIC

Figure 19–1. Points of Contact at the DDN NIC

Once connected to the NIC, you'll receive instructions that list your options. The main options are:

1. issue the command TACNEWS in order to read NIC newsletters
2. issue the command NIC in order to query the online data bases for information on documentation, users of the DDN, and host computers on the DDN

3. issue the command WHOIS or NICNAME in order to directly query the database of registered users of the DDN (the commands "WHOIS HELP" or "NICNAME HELP" provide documentation on how to use this facility)

For the first two options, the procedure is self-explanatory and quite easy to follow.

In addition, NAMSER, the internet host name server, is available on port 101 (decimal) of the NIC. You can access NAMSER by giving the command:

TELNET SRI-NIC 101

NAMSER provides machine-translatable host name, address, and attribute information for networks, gateways, and host computers within the DDN. For instructions on its use, issue the command "HELP" once you've established a connection. For further documentation on NAMSER, see RFC 952 and RFC 953.

19.1.1 TACNEWS

Once you're in contact with the NIC, you can access TACNEWS with the "TACNEWS" command. TACNEWS provides:

1. Login help for MILNET TAC users;
2. The current list of ARPANET and MILNET TAC telephone numbers;
3. A mechanism for reading the DDN Newsletters; and
4. A mechanism for reading the DDN Management Bulletins

All DDN users should read the DDN Newsletters and DDN Management Bulletins in order to stay current on DDN policies, announcments, and news.

19.1.2 NIC/QUERY

The NIC/QUERY system is accessed by the "NIC" command once the user is in contact with the NIC. NIC/QUERY is menu-driven and is oriented toward the novice or casual users of the NIC. NIC/QUERY provides:

1. Access to the database of registered DDN users, allowing the user of NIC/QUERY to look up people on the DDN. For each registered user, his name, network mailing address, US postal address, telephone number, and host computer are maintained in this database.

2. Access to the database host computers for the ARPANET and MILNET. For each host computer, its name and NICnames, network address, physical location, and points of contact for the host administrator and liaison are maintained in this database.

3. Information on the RFC and IEN documents. RFCs (Request For Comments) and IENs (Internet Experiment Notes) document the protocols and tools used in the operation of the DDN.

4. Information on hardcopy documentation available from the NIC and how to acquire this documentation. Many NIC documents are available in hardcopy form, and some are available online.

19.1.3 WHOIS/NICNAME

WHOIS/NICNAME is a program on the NIC which provides an electronic "white pages" of registered DDN users. For each registered user, his name, network mailing address, US postal address, telephone number, and host computer are listed.

19.1.4 Online Directories

The NIC supports the anonymous login convention, allowing DDN users to access files in selected public directories on the NIC. Directories of specific interest are:

1. NETINFO: - contains general information on the DDN,

2. DDN-NEWS: - contains DDN Newsletters and DDN Management Bulletins

3. RFC: - contains RFCs and IENs

Some files of particular interest from these directories are named in Figure 19-2.

Title	*Filename*
ARPANET Information Brochure	NETINFO:AIB.DOC
DDN Management Bulletins	DDN-NEWS:DDN-MGT-BULLETIN-nn.TXT
DDN New User Guide	NETINFO:NUG.DOC
DDN Newsletters	DDN-NEWS:DDN-NEWS-nn.TXT
DDN Publications (Hardcopy)	NETINFO:NIC-PUBS.TXT
Electronic Mailing Lists	NETINFO:INTEREST-GROUPS-1.TXT
	NETINFO:INTEREST-GROUPS-2.TXT
Kermit Documentation	NETINFO:KERMIT-INFO.TXT
	NETINFO:KERMIT-TAC-INFO.TXT
NETINFO Index	NETINFO:00NETINFO-INDEX.TXT
RFC Index	RFC:RFC-INDEX.TXT
RFCs	RFC:RFCnnn.TXT
TAC User's Guide	NETINFO:TAC-USER.DOC

Figure 19–2. Key Files at SRI-NIC

19.2

DDN User Guides

One of the databases presented to the user by the NIC includes information on the DDN User Guides. There are five items in this category.

The *DDN New User Guide* is a nuts-and-bolts guide to the DDN for network users. It describes how to use electronic mail and file transfer and is available in hard copy from the Defense Technical Information Center (DTIC) for a modest price; DTIC Order Number is AD-A166 368.

The *TAC User's Guide* is a guide to using the Terminal Access Controllers (TACs) on the DDN. Included are the TAC commands and features. This document is also available from the DTIC for a modest price; DTIC Order Number is AD-A147 366.

The *DDN Directory* is a directory of users and host computers on the DDN. It shows the name, network mailbox, US mail address, and telephone number of each registered DDN user. This document is also available from the DTIC for a modest price; DTIC Order Number is AD-A148 213.

Military personnel or DoD contractors with the proper authorization may obtain protocol-related documents such as circulars, directives, or memoranda from the Defense Technical Information Center (DTIC). The DTIC's address and telephone number are:

Defense Technical Information Center
Cameron Station
Alexandria, Virginia 22314
(202) 274-7633

19.3

Acquiring RFCs via FTP

Request for Comments (RFCs) are technical notes on the operation of the Defense Data Network, and they are available from the NIC with the aid of FTP and anonymous login. There are hundreds of RFCs, and they are stored in the directory named "RFC:". If you want to scan the RFCs, obtain the key file named

RFC-INDEX.TXT.

RFCs cover a wide variety of topics, including details on the File Transfer Protocol, electronic mail, domain and host computer naming, and host-TAC communications. The RFCs are very detailed.

Figure 19-3 illustrates a connection via FTP to the NIC. Characters typed by the user are in *italics*.

@ftp nic
< SRI-NIC.ARPA FTP Server Process 5Z(46)-6 at Wed
        8-Oct-86 21:55-PDT
Setting default transfer type to paged.
FTP>*login anonymous*
Password:
< User MILNET-FTP logged in at Wed 8-Oct-86
        21:55-PDT, job 16.
FTP>*set stat*
FTP>*get rfc:rfc-inaex.txt*
PS:<RFC>RFC-INDEX.TXT.178 (to local file)
PS:<RFC>RFC-INDEX.TXT.178 =>
        <RCONN>RFC-INDEX.TXT.1;P777700 !!!!! [OK]
Transferred 92870 7-bit bytes (37 pages) in 2:44.8
        seconds, 3.349 CPU
for a total transfer rate of 3 kilobaud.
FTP>*quit*

Figure 19-3. Accessing SRI-NIC via FTP

Chapter 20

Columbia University (CU20B) and Kermit

Kermit is an error-detecting protocol designed to transfer files between a very wide variety of computers over a very wide variety of communications media. Kermit is non-proprietary, thoroughly documented, and in wide use on over 200 different types of computers and operating systems all over the world. Kermit has been widely adopted by users of the Defense Data Network to transfer files between DDN host computers and their local personal computers.

The Kermit protocol and its original implementations were developed at the Columbia University Center for Computing Activities. All Kermit programs perform file transfer using the Kermit file transfer protocol, and many Kermit programs for personal computers also provide terminal emulation, usually for popular terminals like the VT100 of Digital Equipment Corporation. Some of the more popular Kermit implementations are:

- Kermit for the CP/M operating system of Digital Research
- Kermit for the IBM Personal Computer
- Kermit for the Apple Macintosh family
- Kermit for various flavors of the UNIX operating system
- Kermit for the VAX/VMS operating system of Digital Equipment Corporation
- Kermit for IBM mainframes running the VM/CMS and MVS/TSO operating systems

20.1 Kermit on CU20B

Columbia University is the home of Kermit, and the DDN host computer named CU20B contains all of the available Kermit implementations as well as Kermit-related documentation on a variety of topics in the directories named "KER:".

To access this information, the DDN user should log into CU20B via the anonymous login convention under FTP and obtain the file "KER:AAAREAD.ME". This file points to other files which will enable the user to quickly identify the Kermit-related files (and implementations) he is interested in so he can transfer them.

20.2 INFO-KERMIT Electronic Mail

The INFO-KERMIT electronic mailing list is supported by the people at CU20B. This EMail list is a forum for discussion on Kermit-related matters, including new implementations. To subscribe to INFO-KERMIT, send a request via electronic mail to

INFO-KERMIT-REQUEST@CU20B.COLUMBIA.EDU

20.3 Accessing CU20B via FTP

Figure 20-1 shows a sample FTP session in which CU20B is accessed from SIMTEL20. Characters typed by the user are presented in *italics*. The anonymous login convention is used.

```
@ftp cu20b
< CU20B.COLUMBIA.EDU FTP Server Process 5Z(46)-7 at
        Thu 9-Oct-86 00:44-EDT
Setting default transfer type to paged.
FTP>login anonymous
Password:
< User ANONYMOUS logged in at Thu 9-Oct-86 00:44-EDT,
        job 14.
FTP>set stat
FTP>get ker:aaaread.me
WS2:<KERMIT>AAAREAD.ME.4 (to local file)
 WS2:<KERMIT>AAAREAD.ME.4 =>
        <RCONN>AAAREAD.ME.2;P777700 !! [OK]
Transferred 1904 7-bit bytes (1 pages) in 5.9 seconds,
        0.210 CPU
for a total transfer rate of 2 kilobaud.
FTP>quit
```

Figure 20–1. Accessing CU20B via FTP

Chapter 21

ADA20

The DDN host computer known as ADA20 (ADA20.ISI.EDU is its full domain name) is the home of many information files which are of interest to those people who are involved in the Ada effort. These information files may be freely accessed by authorized DDN users only, so this chapter pertains to authorized DDN users only.

The Ada Joint Program Office (AJPO) supports a DDN host computer at the University of Southern California (USC) Information Sciences Institute (ISI). This host computer is ADA20, which is an alias for System F at USC (USC-ISIF). Accounts on this system are controlled by the AJPO and are limited to those individuals "providing a significant level of support to the Ada effort." However, DDN users can access ADA20 and obtain via FTP (using the anonymous login convention) a number of files, as presented below.

21.1 Summary of Directories on ADA20

Some of the directories on ADA20 may be accessed by any DDN user by employing the File Transfer Protocol (FTP) tool and using the anonymous login convention. These directories are:

Directory NameType of Information

<ADA-INFO>
General Ada-Oriented Information

<ARTEWG-INFO>
Ada Runtime Environment Working Group

<EV-INFO>
Evaluation and Validation

<KIT-INFO>
KAPSE Interface Team

<VALIDATION-INFO>
Ada Computer Validation

21.1.1

<ADA-INFO>

The directory named <ADA-INFO> on ADA20 contains information of general interest to the Ada community. The file FILES.HLP identifies each of the files in <ADA-INFO> and gives a brief description of their contents. Some of the files are described in the following paragraphs.

1750A.HLP

contains information on the status of the Sixteen Bit Computer Instruction Set Architecture known as MIL-STD-1750A.

ACVC.HLP

contains information on how to obtain copies of the latest Ada Compiler Validation Capability (ACVC) Test Suite.

ADA-BIB.HLP

contains a description of the Ada Bibliography as well as ordering information.

ADA-CALR.HLP

contains a brief list of upcoming Ada events. Conferences and educational programs are included.

ADA-RBBS.HLP

contains information on how to access the Ada Information Clearinghouse (AdaIC) bulletin board.

ADABOOKS.HLP

contains abstracts of many of the Ada textbooks listed in the file TEXT-BIB.HLP.

ADATODAY.HLP

is Ada* TODAY, an online newsletter which provides current information on people, events, and publications related to the Ada effort.

AJPO-STF.HLP

contains the names, addresses, and phone numbers of the personnel at the Ada Joint Program Office.

ALS-STAT.HLP

contains current updates on the Ada Language System.

CAISUPDT.HLP

contains information regarding the status of the MIL-STD-CAIS (CAIS stands for Common APSE Interface Set, where APSE stands for Ada Programming Support Environment).

CLAS-SEM.HLP

contains a list of upcoming classes, tutorials, workshops, and seminars on the Ada programming language.

CONF-PRO.HLP

contains a list of upcoming conferences and programs on the Ada programming language.

CONTACTS.HLP

contains a list of contacts for Ada information.

DIANA.HLP

contains information on DIANA (the Ada intermediate language) and how to obtain the DIANA reference manual.

DOCU-REF.HLP

contains a list of Ada-related documents and the agencies from which they are available.

GLOSSARY.HLP

contains an alphabetical listing of Ada-related terms and their meanings.

IMPGUIDE.HLP

contains information on how to obtain the revised Ada Compiler Validation Implementer's Guide.

IMPL-MAT.HLP

is a list of Ada language implementations.

ISO-STAT.HLP

contains status reports on the International Standards Organization (ISO).

KAPSE.HLP

contains information on how to obtain the latests KAPSE (Kernel Ada Programming Support Environment) Interface Team (KIT) Public Report.

LRM.HLP

contains instructions on how to obtain a machine-readable copy of the Ada Language Reference Manual (LRM).

METHODMN.HLP

contains status information on the Methodology Area Summary Documents (Methodman II).

NATO-ADA.HLP

contains information on NATO's adoption of Ada as their common high-order language (HOL) in military systems.

NEWSLTR.HLP

contains the most recent issue of the Quarterly AdaIC Newsletter.

TEXT-BIB.HLP

contains a list of Ada language textbooks which is arranged alphabetically by title.

TRADEMRK.HLP

contains guidelines on using the Ada trademark.

VAL-COMP.HLP

contains a current list of validated Ada compilers.

VAL-POL.HLP

contains the draft version of the Ada Validation Policies and Procedures Document.

VALFACIL.HLP

contains a list of the Ada Validation Facilities (AVFs) performing Ada Compiler Validation Capability tests.

21.1.2 <ARTEWG-INFO>

The directory <ARTEWG-INFO> on ADA20 contains files associated with the Ada Runtime Environment Working Group (ARTEWG). This directory contains a file named FILES.HLP which names each file in <ARTEWG-INFO> and summarizes its contents.

21.1.3 <EV-INFO>

The directory <EV-INFO> on ADA20 contains files associated with the Ada Programming Support Environment (APSE) Evaluation and Validation (E&V) Task. The purpose of this task is to develop the techniques and tools which will provide a capability to perform assessment of APSEs and to determine conformance of APSEs to the AJPO-sponsored Common APSE Interface Set (CAIS). As the E&V technology is developed, it will be made available to the community for use by the DoD components, industry, and academia.

<EV-INFO> contains E&V documents and other E&V-related publications. The file FILES.HLP in <EV-INFO> names all the files in <EV-INFO> and summarizes their contents. Some of these files are listed in the following paragraphs.

APSE-QUESTIONS.HLP lists over 400 generic APSE evaluation questions and comments.

COMPILER-CRITERIA.HLP

lists evaluation criteria and associated tests for use in assessing numerous attributes of Ada compilers.

TESTS-ADA-FAIR-84.HLP

contains compiler benchmark tests which the Los Angeles AdaTEC used for the Ada Fair in 1984.

TESTS-ADA-FAIR-85.HLP

contains compiler benchmark tests which the Los Angeles AdaTEC used for the Ada Fair in 1985.

TESTS-SRI.HLP

contains compiler benchmark tests developed by Stanford Research Institute (SRI) to determine how to optimally use tasking, rendezvous, selects, and parameter passing.

21.1.4 <KIT-INFO>

The directory <KIT-INFO> contains information on the KAPSE (Kernel Ada Programming Support Environment) Interface Team (KIT). Much documentation on MIL-STD-CAIS (CAIS is the Common APSE Interface Set, where APSE is Ada Programming Support Environment) is located here.

The file FILES.HLP lists the names of files contained in <KIT-INFO> along with brief descriptions of their contents.

21.1.5 <VALIDATION-INFORMATION>

Information on the Ada compiler validation effort is contained in the directory <VALIDATION-INFORMATION> on ADA20.

21.2 The INFO-ADA EMail List

The INFO-ADA Electronic Mailing list is maintained on ADA20. This mailing list is used as a general form for the discussion of any Ada-related matters and for raising questions on Ada-related topics. Many experts on Ada subscribe to the list, and all questions are addressed.

To subscribe to the INFO-ADA EMail list, send a request via electronic mail to:

INFO-ADA-REQUEST@ADA20.ISI.EDU

ADA-SW is another Electronic Mailing list, but it is maintained on SIMTEL20 and is dedicated to users of the Ada Software Repository. ADA-SW is discussed in the section on the Ada Software Repository.

21.3 Accessing ADA20 via FTP

Figure 21-1 shows a sample FTP session in which ADA20 is accessed from SIMTEL20. Characters typed by the user are presented in *italics*. The anonymous login convention is used.

```
@ftp ada20
< ADA20.ISI.EDU FTP Server Process 5Z(27)-7 at Wed
        8-Oct-86 21:39-PDT
Setting default transfer type to paged.
FTP>login anonymous
Password:
< User ANONYMOUS logged in at Wed 8-Oct-86 21:40-PDT,
        job 17.
FTP>set stat
FTP>get <ada-info>files.hlp ada-files.hlp
 PS:<ADA-INFO>FILES.HLP.47
        => <RCONN>ADA-FILES.HLP.1;P777700 !! [OK]
Transferred 12372 7-bit bytes (5 pages) in 10.6 seconds,
        0.522 CPU
for a total transfer rate of 8 kilobaud.
FTP>get <ev-info>files.hlp ev-files.hlp
 PS:<EV-INFO>FILES.HLP.33
        => <RCONN>EV-FILES.HLP.1;P777700 !! [OK]
Transferred 6509 7-bit bytes (3 pages) in 5.3 seconds, 0.335 CPU
for a total transfer rate of 8 kilobaud.
FTP>quit
```

Figure 21-1. Accessing ADA20 via FTP

Chapter 22

Electronic Mailing Lists on the DDN

One of the most significant resources available to users of the Defense Data Network is electronic mail. A DDN user can send electronic messages to any other DDN user or electronic bulletin board, to special mail server programs (discussed later), and to electronic mailing lists.

An electronic mailing list is a list of addresses of people interested in a particular topic. By sending an electronic mail message to the address of the list itself (e.g., sending mail to ADA-SW@SIMTEL20), a mail server receives the message, realizes that the message is addressed to an electronic mailing list, and transmits duplicates of the message to each address on that electronic mailing list. An address on an electronic mailing list may be that of an individual or of another electronic mailing list, and the message can be rapidly distributed to thousands of mailing list subscribers.

Some electronic mailing lists are completely open. When you send a message to the list, it goes to the mail server itself, and the message is typically retransmitted as soon as it is received. Other electronic mailing lists are moderated. When you send a message to a moderated list, it goes to a person who acts as the moderator of the list. The moderator may respond in several ways, depending upon how he chose to run the mailing list.

One way a moderator may run an electronic mailing list is to collect all messages received during a certain time period, such as one day, and concatenate these messages into one large message which he then sends to the mail server for the list. The subscribers to this type of list then receive only one large message during a time period rather than many smaller messages at irregular intervals. Such combined messages are called digests. HUMAN-NETS and "Computers and Society Digest" are examples of electronic mailing lists which transmit digests.

A second way a moderator may run an electronic mailing list is to read each message submitted and approve or disapprove its redistribution to the list. If the message is approved, he may send it out individually or as a part of a digest, again depending on how the list is set up. ARPANET-BBOARDS is an example of an electronic mailing list in which each message is evaluated by a moderator before being distributed to the list.

The vast majority of electronic mailing lists on the Defense Data Network are completely open.

22.1 Getting Started with an Electronic Mailing List

The convention for handling administrative matters concerning an electronic mailing list (such as subscribing to the list, requesting to be dropped from the list, and asking about archive files of previous messages) is to send electronic mail messages to the REQUEST address for the list. This address usually takes the form of "list-REQUEST@host" (such as ADA-SW-REQUEST@SIMTEL20 for the ADA-SW electronic mailing list distributed from the host computer named SIMTEL20, or INFO-IBMPC-REQUEST@USC-ISIB for the INFO-IBMPC electronic mailing list distributed from the host computer named USC-ISIB). Messages sent to the REQUEST address are read by the moderator or mailing list maintainer rather than by the entire membership of the list.

The moderator or maintainer personally acts on the messages.

22.2 Selected Electronic Mail Lists

The number of electronic mailing lists on the DDN is constantly growing, and the Network Information Center attempts to track these lists and provide information to the DDN users on the status of these lists. To this end, the NETINFO: directory contains files named INTEREST-GROUPS-1.TXT and INTEREST-GROUPS-2.TXT which describe the subjects and intended audiences of the electronic mailing lists, and how to subscribe. Also, an electronic mailing list is maintained to notify interested parties when these files are updated.

Electronic mailing lists whose subjects fall into the following categories are documented on the following pages. The categories are:

Ada
Artificial Intelligence
Computer Programming Languages Other than Ada
Computer Networking and Communications
Computer Systems Other than Personal Computers
Personal Computers
Politics and Society
Space
Workstations

22.2.1 Ada

Electronic Mailing List: ADA-SW

Description: ADA-SW is a mailing list for people who are interested in accessing the software in, and contributing software to, the Ada Software Repository on SIMTEL20. This list serves two purposes: (1) to support information exchange between repository users, including announcements of the release of new software and bug reports on existing software, and (2) to mail submissions to the Ada Software Repository for inclusion in the repository.

List Administration:

ADA-SW-REQUEST@SIMTEL20.ARPA

Electronic Mailing List: INFO-ADA

Description: INFO-ADA is for announcements, questions and discussions of a technical nature, requests for information, and anything else having to do with the Ada programming language (ANSI/MIL-STD-1815A-1983).

List Administration:

INFO-ADA-REQUEST@ADA20.ISI.EDU

22.2.2

Artificial Intelligence

Electronic Mailing List: AI-ED

Description: AI-ED supports discussions related to the application of artificial intelligence to education. Subjects include intelligent computer assisted instruction (ICAI), intelligent tutoring systems (ITS), interactive encyclopedias, intelligent information retrieval for educational purposes, psychological and cognitive science models of learning, problem solving, and teaching that can be applied to education, and issues related to teaching Artificial Intelligence.

List Administration:

AI-Ed-Request@SUMEX-AIM.ARPA

Electronic Mailing List: AIList

Description: AIList supports the discussion of artificial intelligence and related topics:

Expert Systems	AI Techniques
Knowledge Representation	Knowledge Acquisition
Problem Solving	Hierarchical Inference
Machine Learning	Pattern Recognition
Analogical Reasoning	Data Analysis
Cognitive Psychology	Human Perception
AI Languages and Systems	Machine Translation
Theorem Proving	Decision Theory
Logic Programming	Automatic Programming

Messages range from tutorials to speculation. The following types of messages are encouraged:

Abstracts	Reviews
Lab Descriptions	Research Overviews
Work Planned or In Progress	Bibliographies
Conference Announcements	Conference Reports
Puzzles and Unsolved Problems	Queries and Requests

List Administration:

AIList-Request@SRI-AI.ARPA

Electronic Mailing List: NL-KR

Description: NL-KR supports the discussion of any topic related to natural language (both understanding and generation) and knowledge representation. Primary topics are:

Knowledge Representation	Natural Language Understanding
Discourse Understanding	Philosophy of Language
Plan Recognition	Computational Linguistics

Secondary topics include:

Cognitive Psychology	Human Perception
Linguistics	Machine Translation

List Administration:

NL-KR-REQUEST@ROCHESTER.ARPA

Electronic Mailing List: PARSYM

Description: PARSYM supports discussions on parallel symbolic computing (non-numeric computing using multiple processors). Topics relate to parallelism in symbolic computing and to the use of symbolic computing techniques (AI objects, logic programming, expert systems) in parallel computing.

List Administration:

PARSYM-Request@SUMEX-AIM.ARPA

Electronic Mailing List: VISION-LIST

Description: VISION-LIST supports discussions on vision research in the AI arena. Topics include physiological theory, computer vision, AI technology applied to vision research, machine vision algorithms, industrial applications, robotic eyes, and anything related to vision and its automation.

List Administration:

Vision-List-Request@ADS.ARPA

22.2.3

Computer Programming Languages Other than Ada

Electronic Mailing List: ASM370

Description: ASM370 supports discussion of and questions about programming in IBM System/370 Assembly Language and the distribution of programs.

List Administration:

EDITOR%UCF1VM.BITNET@WISCVM.WISC.EDU

Electronic Mailing List: BIZARRE-PEOPLE

Description: BIZARRE-PEOPLE is a forum for the discussion of recursive descent parsing and related methods. Parsers for applicative languages are emphasized.

List Administration:

BIZARRE-PEOPLE- REQUEST@PT.CS.CMU.EDU

Electronic Mailing List: FIGIL

Description: FIGIL is the FORTH Interest Groups International List. The FORTH computer language is discussed. Software distribution is supported.

List Administration:

UMFORTH%WEIZMANN.BITNET@WISCVM.WISC.EDU

Electronic Mailing List: FRANZ-FRIENDS

Description: FRANZ-FRIENDS discusses the Franz LISP Language.

List Administration:

FRANZ-FRIENDS@BERKELEY

Electronic Mailing List: Icon-Group

Description: Icon-Group discusses topics related to the Icon programming language.

List Administration:

Icon-Group- Request%Arizona.CSNET@CSNET-RELAY.ARPA

Electronic Mailing List: INFO-C

Description: INFO-C discusses the C programming language.

List Administration:

INFO-C-REQUEST@BRL.ARPA

Electronic Mailing List: INFO-IDL

Description: INFO-IDL discusses the IDL (Interface Design Language) and IDL-like technologies.

List Administration:

INFO-IDL-REQUEST@SEI.CMU.EDU

Electronic Mailing List: INFO-MACFORTH

Description: INFO-MACFORTH discusses the MacFORTH programming environment.

List Administration:

INFO-MACFORTH-REQUEST@HARVARD.ARPA

Electronic Mailing List: INFO-MODULA-2

Description: INFO-MODULA-2 discusses the Modula-2 programming language.

List Administration:

INFO-MODULA-2-
REQUEST@ROCHESTER.ARPA

Electronic Mailing List: INFO-PASCAL

Description: INFO-PASCAL discusses the Pascal programming language.

List Administration:

INFO-PASCAL-REQUEST@BRL.ARPA

Electronic Mailing List: INFO-XLISP

Description: INFO-XLISP discusses the XLISP language and provides a forum for code exchange.

List Administration:

INFO-XLISP-REQUEST@PT.CS.CMU.EDU

Electronic Mailing List: LINGUA

Description: LINGUA discusses all aspects of Computer Programming Languages.

List Administration:

EDITOR%UCF1VM.BITNET@WISCVM.WISC.EDU

Electronic Mailing List: PROLOG

Description: PROLOG and PROLOG-HACKERS discuss Prolog and logic programming. PROLOG is a moderated digest, and PROLOG-HACKERS is an open mailing list of the same material.

List Administration:

PROLOG-REQUEST@SCORE.ARPA

Electronic Mailing List: SCHEME

Description: SCHEME discusses the Scheme programming language with emphasis on the use of Scheme in education.

List Administration:

Scheme-Request@MC.LCS.MIT.EDU

Electronic Mailing List: VPLLIST

Description: VPLLIST discusses the study, design, development, implementation, and evaluation of visual programming languages (VPLs).

List Administration:

VPLLIST-REQUEST@SU-SUSHI.ARPA

22.2.4 Computer Networking and Communications

Electronic Mailing List: ARPA-MHS

Description: ARPA-MHS discusses gatewaying of ARPA RFC920 addresses with MHS X.400 addresses.

List Administration:

ARPA-MHS-REQUEST@BRL.ARPA

Electronic Mailing List: HEADER-PEOPLE

Description: HEADER-PEOPLE discusses the formats of message headers and related issues, including internetwork mail formats and standards.

List Administration:

HEADER-PEOPLE-REQUEST@AI.AI.MIT.EDU

Electronic Mailing List: IBM-NETS

Description: IBM-NETS discusses IBM mainframes and networking them.

List Administration:

Hank%BITNIC.BITNET@WISCVM.WISC.EDU

Electronic Mailing List: INFO-KERMIT

Description: INFO-KERMIT distributes information on the Kermit file transfer protocol and its implementations.

List Administration:

INFO-KERMIT-REQUEST@CU20B.ARPA

Electronic Mailing List: INFO-NETS

Description: INFO-NETS gathers information on the BITNET and other networks. Specific questions about specific networks are addressed.

List Administration:

INFO-NETS-REQUEST%MIT-
OZ@MC.LCS.MIT.EDU

Electronic Mailing List: INFO-PCNET

Description: INFO-PCNET discusses PCNET, a computer network for personal use.

List Administration:

INFO-PCNET-REQUEST@MC.LCS.MIT.EDU

Electronic Mailing List: INFO-TMODEM

Description: INFO-TMODEM distributes information to users of TMODEM.

List Administration:

INFO-TMODEM-REQUEST@SIMTEL20.ARPA

Electronic Mailing List: INFO-XMODEM

Description: INFO-XMODEM discusses the XMODEM, or Christensen, file transfer protocol.

List Administration:

INFO-XMODEM-REQUEST@SIMTEL20.ARPA

Electronic Mailing List: lan-news

Description: lan-news discusses implementation details of netnews over local area networks.

List Administration:

lan-news-request@SDCSVAX.UCSD.EDU

Electronic Mailing List: MH-USERS

Description: MH-USERS discusses the UCI version of the Rand Message Handling (MH) system.

List Administration:

MH-Users-Request@UCI.ARPA

Electronic Mailing List: MMM-PEOPLE

Description: MMM-PEOPLE discusses multimedia electronic mail.

List Administration:

WESTINE@USC-ISIB.ARPA

Electronic Mailing List: NAMEDROPPERS

Description: NAMEDROPPERS discusses the concepts, principles, design, and implementation of the domain-style names.

List Administration:

NAMEDROPPERS@SRI-NIC.ARPA

Electronic Mailing List: PACKET-RADIO

Description: PACKET-RADIO discusses packet radio.

List Administration:

PACKET-RADIO-REQUEST@MIT-EDDIE.ARPA

Electronic Mailing List: PC-Token-Ring

Description: PC-Token-Ring discusses the IBM PC token ring.

List Administration:

PC-Token-Ring-Request@UCLA-CCN.ARPA

Electronic Mailing List: PCIP

Description: PCIP discusses TCP/IP and its implementations.

List Administration:

PCIP-REQUEST@LOUIE.UDEL.EDU

Electronic Mailing List: ProtocolS

Description: ProtocolS discusses various existing FTP protocols.

List Administration:

ProtocolS-REQUEST@RUTGERS.ARPA

Electronic Mailing List: SERVERS

Description: SERVERS discusses network (primarily BITNET) and internetwork file servers.

List Administration:

EDITOR%UCF1VM.BITNET@WISCVM.WISC.EDU

Electronic Mailing List: TCP-IP

Description: TCP-IP provides information on TCP-IP implementations from the Network Information Center.

List Administration:

TCP-IP-REQUEST@SRI-NIC.ARPA

Electronic Mailing List: TELECOM

Description: TELECOM is a digest which discusses telecommunications technology, particularly the telephone system, modems, and technical aspects thereof.

List Administration:

TELECOM-REQUEST@XX.LCS.MIT.EDU

Electronic Mailing List: V2LNI-PEOPLE

Description: V2LNI-PEOPLE discusses Pronet/V2LNI Ring networks.

List Administration:

LWA@MC.LCS.MIT.EDU

22.2.5

Computer Systems Other than Personal Computers and Workstations

Electronic Mailing List: Cyber-L

Description: Cyber-L is a digest for people who support or install Control Data (CDC) systems.

List Administration:

Info%Bitnic.BITNET@WISCVM.WISC.EDU

Electronic Mailing List: INFO-AOS

Description: INFO-AOS is for Data General's AOS/VS operating system and the computers on which it runs.

List Administration:

INFO-AOS-REQUEST@SU-SIERRA

Electronic Mailing List: INFO-PYRAMID

Description: INFO-PYRAMID discusses Pyramid computers.

List Administration:

mark@MARYLAND

Electronic Mailing List: INFO-RIDGE

Description: INFO-RIDGE discusses the Ridge 32 computer and the ROS operating system.

List Administration:

INFO-RIDGE-REQUEST@HOPKINS-EECS-BRAVO.ARPA

Electronic Mailing List: INFO-RSTS

Description: INFO-RSTS discusses topics related to the RSTS/E operating system for the PDP-11.

List Administration:

INFO-RSTS-REQUEST%MIT-OZ@MC.LCS.MIT.EDU

Electronic Mailing List: INFO-SEQUENT

Description: INFO-SEQUENT discusses computers made by Sequent Computer Systems, Inc. The Balance 8000 is discussed in particular.

List Administration:

INFO-SEQUENT- REQUEST@IM4U.UTEXAS.EDU

Electronic Mailing List: INFO-VAX

Description: INFO-VAX discusses the VAX series of computers by Digital Equipment Corporation.

List Administration:

INFO-VAX-REQUEST@SRI-KL.ARPA

Electronic Mailing List: MER.SIGBIG

Description: MER.SIGBIG discusses supercomputers.

List Administration:

JUP.WELCH@AMES-VMSB.ARPA

Electronic Mailing List: MUS

Description: MUS (Masscomp Users Society) discusses the Masscomp line of computers.

List Administration:

MUS-REQUEST@ENEEVAX.UMD.EDU

22.2.6 Personal Computers

Electronic Mailing List: CBMLIST

Description: CBMLIST is for users of all 8-bit Commodore computers, including PET, CBM, B128, VIC-20, Commodore 64, and Commodore 128.

List Administration:

MKimmel%UMass.BITNET@WISCVM.WISC.EDU

Electronic Mailing List: HEATH-PEOPLE

Description: HEATH-PEOPLE is for users of Heath terminals and computers and related Zenith products.

List Administration:

HEATH-PEOPLE-REQUEST@MC.LCS.MIT.EDU

Electronic Mailing List: INFO-AMIGA

Description: INFO-AMIGA is for users of the Amiga PC from Commodore Business Machines.

List Administration:

INFO-AMIGA-REQUEST@RUTGERS.ARPA

Electronic Mailing List: INFO-APPLE

Description: INFO-APPLE is for users of Apple computers.

List Administration:

INFO-APPLE-REQUEST@BRL.ARPA

Electronic Mailing List: INFO-ATARI16

Description: INFO-ATARI16 is for users of the 16-bit Atari computer family.

List Administration:

INFO-ATARI-REQUEST@SU-SCORE.ARPA

Electronic Mailing List: INFO-ATARI8

Description: INFO-ATARI8 is for users of the 8-bit Atari computer family.

List Administration:

INFO-ATARI-REQUEST@SU-SCORE.ARPA

Electronic Mailing List: INFO-CPM

Description: INFO-CPM is for users of all computers running all 8- and 16-bit CP/M operating systems.

List Administration:

INFO-CPM-REQUEST@AMSAA.ARPA

Electronic Mailing List: INFO-DEC-MICRO

Description: INFO-DEC-MICRO is for users of microcomputers manufactured by Digital Equipment Corporation. These include the Rainbow 100, the MicroVAX, and the Professional 350/380.

List Administration:

Info-DEC-Micro-Request@SU- SCORE.ARPA

Electronic Mailing List: INFO-HZ100

Description: INFO-HZ100 is for users of the Zenith Z-100 (Heath H-100) family of personal computers.

List Administration:

INFO-HZ100-REQUEST@RADC-TOPS20.ARPA

Electronic Mailing List: INFO-IBMPC

Description: INFO-IBMPC is for users of the IBM Personal Computer family and the compatibles.

List Administration:

INFO-IBMPC-REQUEST@USC-ISIB.ARPA

Electronic Mailing List: INFO-LAPTOPS

Description: INFO-LAPTOPS is for users of laptop portable personal computers.

List Administration:

INFO-LAPTOPS%MIT-OZ@MC.LCS.MIT.EDU

Electronic Mailing List: INFO-MAC

Description: INFO-MAC is for users of the Apple Macintosh computer.

List Administration:

INFO-MAC-REQUEST@SUMEX-AIM.ARPA

Electronic Mailing List: INFO-MICRO

Description: INFO-MICRO is for discussions of microcomputers in general.

List Administration:

INFO-MICRO-REQUEST@BRL.ARPA

Electronic Mailing List: INFO-XENIX310

Description: INFO-XENIX310 is for users of Xenix on the Intel 310s.

List Administration:

INFO-XENIX310-REQUEST@SIMTEL20.ARPA

Electronic Mailing List: Mail-Zilog

Description: Mail-Zilog is for users of Zilog computers and the Zeus operating system.

List Administration:

cbmvax!mail-zilog@SEISMO.CSS.GOV

Electronic Mailing List: NORTHSTAR-USERS

Description: NORTHSTAR-USERS is for users of Northstar microcomputers.

List Administration:

NORTHSTAR-USERS-
REQUEST@SIMTEL20.ARPA

22.2.7

Politics and Society

Electronic Mailing List: ARMS-D

Description: ARMS-D is a digest of comments and questions on United States policy issues related to peace, war, national security, weapons, the arms race, and similar topics.

List Administration:

ARMS-D-REQUEST@XX.LCS.MIT.EDU

Electronic Mailing List: Computers and Society Digest

Description: Computers and Society Digest discusses issues related to the impact of technology and information on society. Significant issues include:

Computers and Social Responsibility
Dealing with Information Overload
The Classed Society in the Information Age
Public Perceptions of Computers
The Value of Information
Dangers and Advantages of Reliance on Machines
Risks of Technological Dependence

List Administration:

taylor@HPLABS.ARPA

Electronic Mailing List: HUMAN-NETS

Description: HUMAN-NETS is a digest which discusses an array of topics related to the theme of a world-wide computer and telecommunications network, usually called WorldNet. Discussions have included tutorials, the state-of-the-art, and technology and its impact on society.

List Administration:

HUMAN-NETS-REQUEST@RUTGERS.ARPA

Electronic Mailing List: INFO-FUTURES

Description: INFO-FUTURES is a digest which discusses current and likely events in technology and their effects on the near future in computing and related areas. Topics of interest include developments in both computing research and industry which may affect decisions on current issues in society.

List Administration:

INFO-FUTURES-REQUEST%BU-CS@CSNET-RELAY.ARPA

Electronic Mailing List: INFO-JAPAN

Description: INFO-JAPAN discusses everything Japanese except the language. Information about Japanese technology, cultural events, politics, and their impact on the United States is presented.

List Administration:

INFO-JAPAN-REQUEST@MC.LCS.MIT.EDU

Electronic Mailing List: INFO-LAW

Description: INFO-LAW is a moderated list which discusses computers and the law.

List Administration:

INFO-LAW-REQUEST@BRL.ARPA

Electronic Mailing List: NUKE-WINTER

Description: NUKE-WINTER distributes information on the nuclear winter phenomenon.

List Administration:

nuke-winter-request%plaid@SUN.ARPA

Electronic Mailing List: POLI-SCI

Description: POLI-SCI is a digest on political science. It was spun off from HUMAN-NETS.

List Administration:

POLI-SCI-REQUEST@RUTGERS.ARPA

Electronic Mailing List: RISKS

Description: RISKS is a moderated list discussing issues related to risks to the public in the use of computer systems. RISKS is sponsored by the ACM Committee on Computers and Public Policy.

List Administration:

RISKS@SRI-CSL.ARPA

Electronic Mailing List: SECURITY

Description: SECURITY is a moderated list which discusses security in general, including electronic, physical, and computer-related security.

List Administration:

SECURITY-REQUEST@RUTGERS

22.2.8

Space

Electronic Mailing List: Astronomy Events

Description: Astronomy Events announces astronomical events and meetings for astronomy groups.

List Administration:

koolish@BBN-UNIX.ARPA

Electronic Mailing List: L-5 Interest Group

Description: The L-5 Interest Group distributes information to L5 members.

List Administration:

ssc-vax!marla@UW-BEAVER.ARPA

Electronic Mailing List: SKY-FANS

Description: SKY-FANS discusses items of interest to amateur observational astronomers.

List Administration:

SWG@XX.LCS.MIT.EDU

Electronic Mailing List: SPACE

Description: SPACE is a digest on space-related topics.

List Administration:

SPACE-REQUEST@MC.LCS.MIT.EDU

22.2.9 Workstations

Electronic Mailing List: APOLLO

Description: APOLLO is for users of Apollo computers.

List Administration:

Apollo-Request@YALE.ARPA

Electronic Mailing List: INFO-1100

Description: INFO-1100 is for users of Xerox 1100 workstations.

List Administration:

Info-1100-Request@SUMEX-AIM.STANFORD.EDU

Electronic Mailing List: INFO-IRIS

Description: INFO-IRIS is for users of Silicon Graphics Iris workstations.

List Administration:

Info-Iris-Request@SUMEX- AIM.STANFORD.EDU

Electronic Mailing List: INFO-TI-EXPLORER

Description: INFO-TI-EXPLORER is for users of the Explorer of Texas Instruments.

List Administration:

INFO-TI-EXPLORER@SUMEX-AIM.STANFORD.EDU

Electronic Mailing List: WorkS

Description: WorkS is for users of personal workstations in general.

List Administration:

WorkS-Request@RUTGERS

APPENDICES

– Outline –

Notes

Glossary of Terms

The following are terms and acronyms used in this book. Definitions are given for terms, whereas organizational acronyms are generally just expanded to their full length. Some useful terms encountered in the use of the DDN are also included.

Ada	The DoD-standard high-order programming language for embedded computer applications.
ADA20	A DDN host computer at USC supported by the AJPO.
AJPO	Ada Joint Program Office.
AMC	ARPANET Network Monitoring Center, located at BBNCC, Cambridge, MA.
APSE	Ada Programming Support Environment.
ARPA	*see* DARPA.
ARPANET	DARPA's packet-switched host-to-host digital communications network which links a wide variety of DoD-sponsored computers at research centers around the world.
ASCII	American Standard Code for Information Interchange.
ASR	Ada Software Repository.
BBN	Bolt Beranek and Newman.
BBNCC	Bolt Beranek and Newman Communications Corporation; the company that provides network

	node hardware, software and field servicing, and manages the ARPANET Network Monitoring Center. Early contributor to the development of the DDN.
backbone	The nodes (see below) and the leased telephone lines and satellites connecting them, which form the core of the DDN.
BITNET	Because It's Time NETwork. A computer network serving over 1300 host computers located at several hundred sites (mostly universities and research centers) in 21 countries.
BTW	By The Way (network slang).
CAIS	Common APSE Interface Set.
CCG	DCA Configuration Control Group, the group which screens and approves changes to the backbone configuration as needed.
CSNET	Computer Science NETwork. The purpose of CSNET is to facilitate research and advanced development in computer science by providing a means for collaboration among those working in the field. Electronic mail is the main service supported. CSNET extends to the United States, Canada, Australia, France, Germany, Israel, Japan, Korea, Sweden, and the United Kingdom. There are about 180 CSNET host computers.
CU20B	A DDN host computer at Columbia University. The Kermit archives are stored there. See Kermit.
DARPA	Defense Advanced Research Projects Agency.

DCA	Defense Communications Agency.
DCEC	Defense Communications Engineering Center.
DDN	Defense Data Network; the DoD's host-to-host, packet- switched data communications network. The DDN interconnects several military networks, one of which is the ARPANET.
DDN PMO	Defense Data Network' Program Management Office; the office within the DCA responsible for management of the DDN.
DECCO	Defense Commercial Communications Office.
DECSYSTEM-20	A 36-bit mainframe computer manufactured by Digital Equipment Corporation. See TOPS-20.
DoD	Department of Defense.
Easynet	An internal engineering network at Digital Equipment Corporation.
EBCDIC	Extended Binary Coded Decimal Interchange Code.
FTP	File Transfer Protocol; the network protocol that allows host-to-host file transfer across the network without disrupting the format of the file being transferred.
gateway	A special computer which interconnects two networks, performs any needed protocol conversion or address translation, and administers access control between them.
HAdmin	Host Administrator; see Appendix for a list of Host Administrator duties.
host	Computer directly connected to a PSN port on the DDN.

HOSTMASTER Mailbox at the NIC for host registration, name, address, and other changes to information in the DDN host table.

hostname Name which officially identifies a host computer attached to the DDN.

IMP Interface Message Processor; now called Packet Switch Node or PSN, which see.

Internet Protocol Standard that allows Internet networks running different protocols to connect and communicate with each other.

IPTO Information Processing Techniques Office; the DARPA office that administers and sets policy for the ARPANET.

ISI University of Southern California Information Sciences Institute.

Kermit A popular communications protocol for transferring files between DDN mainframes and personal microcomputers. Kermit was developed by Columbia University.

LAN Local Area Network; a private network that connects data processing equipment in a limited geographic area (e.g. an office, building, or complex of buildings).

MINET Military Intelligence NETwork.

MIT Massachusetts Institute of Technology.

MIL-STD Military Standard; the specification for a standard (including network protocols) that is to be implemented for a military system or as a product used by the DoD.

MILNET Unclassified operational MILitary NETwork, which is part of the DDN.

MITRE	MITRE Corporation.
NCD	Network Change Directive.
NCR	Network Change Request.
NIC	Network Information Center located at SRI International, Menlo Park, CA, under contract to the DDN PMO.
node	Packet switch; a PSN, TAC, mail bridge, or combination of these.
NRI	National Research Internet. Now being planned by a network working group of White House committees. NRI will interconnect networks owned by the various federal agencies.
NSC	Node Site Coordinator; local DDN representative assigned to a TAC or PSN who is responsible for access control and accountability for all DDN-owned hardware, software and circuits located at the node site. (See Appendix for a list of NSC duties).
OSD	Office of the Secretary of Defense.
PDC	Program Designator Code; code used to identify the funding activity responsible for reimbursing the cost of backbone charges.
PMO	Program Management Office of the DDN.
POC	Point Of Contact.
PSN	Packet Switch Node; a store-and-forward packet switch to which several host computers can be connected.
REGISTRAR	Mailbox at the NIC for user registration, name, address, and other changes to information in the registration (WHOIS) database.

RFC	Requests For Comments; a set of technical notes describing networking research carried out by the DARPA network community (available from the NIC).
RP	Responsible Person; person appointed by DARPA to register ARPANET TAC users in a particular organization.
SIMTEL20	SIMulation and TELeprocessing DECSYSTEM-20. This is the DDN host computer which serves as a home for the Ada Software Repository and eight other software repositories.
site	Organization or facility where host or node equipment is located.
SMTP	Simple Mail Transfer Protocol; the official DoD mail protocol.
socket	Logical address of a port providing access to a specific device or service on a host.
SRI-NIC	The DDN Network Information Center host computer, located at SRI International, Menlo Park, CA. This host is multi-homed on both the ARPANET and the MILNET, and provides information services to both.
SRI	SRI International; location of the DDN Network Information Center and early contributor to the development of the ARPANET and the DDN.
subscriber	A system connected to the ARPANET, and the individuals responsible for that system.
TAC	Terminal Access Controller; a special host attached to a PSN that lets terminals connect directly to the DDN.

TAC Access Code	Password assigned to TAC users for TAC login.
TAC USER ID	Alphanumeric character string that identifies a TAC user upon TAC login.
TCP/IP	Transmission Control Protocol/Internet Protocol; two of the DoD standard network protocols.
TELCO	Telephone company.
TELNET	DoD protocol for opening a transparent (virtual terminal) connection from one host to another. Also refers to the program implementation that provides this service.
TIP	Terminal Interface Processor; predecessor of the TAC, serving a similar function.
TOPS-20	An operating system marketed by Digital Equipment Corporation for use on its DECSYSTEM-20 mainframes. SIMTEL20, ADA20, and SRI-NIC are DEC-20's running TOPS-20. See DECSYSTEM-20.
TSR	Telecommunications Service Request; a valid, approved and funded telecommunications service requirement submitted by DCA through DECCO to the telephone companies.
UCL	University College London, England.
UCLA	University of California, Los Angeles.
UDB	User Database Tool for registering ARPANET users for TAC Access.
USC	University of Southern California.
USENET	A network of over 2000 UNIX systems supported by the UUCP

	and X.25 (and other) communications protocols. The host computers are connected via dial-up telephone lines. Mailing lists, bulletin boards, software repositories, and a news service are some of the facilities supported on USENET.
USR	Unsatisfactory Service Report; report sent to the DDN PMO by a network subscriber to report unsatisfactory network service.
UUCP	UNIX to UNIX CoPy. A file transport service used over dial-ups between adjacent UNIX computers. UUCP is one of the main protocols supporting the USENET.
VNET	The main internal network at IBM. Formed by two distinct networks (RSCS, Remote Spooling and Communications Subsystem, and PVM, Passthru VM), VNET supports mail transfer, file transfer, and remote login. RSCS currently has about 2200 nodes, and PVM has about 1100 nodes.
WSMR	White Sands Missile Range.
XMODEM	A popular communications protocol for microcomputers. Implementations exist for file transfer between DDN mainframes and personal microcomputers.

Further Reading

B.1 Ada Software Repository

Conn, *Ada Software Repository Master Index*, 1986 (Richard Conn), published by Echelon, Inc., 885 N. San Antonio Road, Los Altos, CA 94022, 415/948-3820.

Conn, ASR Newsletters, available for hardcopy subscription from Echelon and also available in the Ada Software Repository (PD:<ADA.NEWS>).

B.2 On Computer Networks, Introductions

Carlson, "Bit-Oriented Data Link Control Procedures", *IEEE Transactions on Communications*, Volume COM-28, Number 4, April 1980.

Cerf and Kirstein, "Issues in Packet-Network Interconnection", *Proceedings of the IEEE*, Volume 66, Number 11, November 1978.

Enslow, "What is a 'Distributed' Data Processing System?", *Computer*, January 1978.

Kleinrock, "Principles and Lessons in Packet Communications", *Proceedings of the IEEE*, Volume 66, Number 11, November 1978.

Postel, "Internetwork Protocol Approaches", *IEEE Transactions on Communications*, April 1980.

Quarterman and Hoskins, "Notable Computer Networks", *Communications of the ACM*, Volume 29, Number 10, October 1986, pp 932 to 971.

Roberts, "The Evolution of Packet Switching", *Proceedings of the IEEE*, Volume 66, Number 11, November 1978.

Scherr, "Distributed Data Processing", *IBM Systems Journal*, Volume 17, Number 4, 1978.

Tanenbaum, *Computer Networks*, Prentice-Hall, 1981, 517 pages.

B.3

Files from the DDN Network Information Center

NETINFO: 00NETINFO-INDEX.TXT

This file is an index to all files in the NETINFO: directory at the Network Information Center (SRI-NIC).

NETINFO: AIB.DOC

This file is the "ARPANET Information Brochure", dated December, 1985, by Stephen Dennett, Elizabeth Feinler, and Francine Perillo. AIB.DOC includes sections on ARPANET management and policies, subscriber access procedures, ARPANET protocols, the network information services provided by the Network Information Center, and key contacts.

NETINFO: ARPA-TACACS.GUIDE

This file is a "Guide to the TAC User Database Tool" by Bolt Beranek and Newman. It describes the TACACS (TAC Access Control System).

NETINFO: HOSTS.TXT

This file lists all DDN Internet host computers (it is over 120 pages long).

NETINFO: IEN-INDEX.TXT

This file is an index to all existing Internet Experiment Notes (IENs). The IEN number, author, date, and subject are presented.

NETINFO: INTEREST-GROUPS-1.TXT and INTEREST-GROUPS-2.TXT

These files name all electronic mailing lists on the Internet which are known to the Network Information Center.

NETINFO: INTERNET.GATEWAYS

This file lists all Internet gateways connected to the Defense Data Network.

NETINFO: SAM-INFO.TXT

This file describes PC SAM, an electronic mail system which can run on IBM PCs and compatibles and interface with mail systems on the DDN.

NETINFO: TAC-USER.DOC

This file is BBN Report Number 4780, the "TAC User's Guide", dated September 1982 and written by Bolt Beranek and Newman.

B.4

RFCs from the DDN Network Information Center

NETINFO: RFC-INDEX.DOC

This file is an index to all RFCs. It is in reverse chronological order, and is over 40 pages long.

All RFCs are located in the directory RFC: at SRI-NIC.

RFC-961, *Official ARPA-Internet Protocols*, by J. Reynolds and J. Postel, dated December 1985. This RFC identifies the official protocols and the documents specifying the official protocols used in the Internet.

RFC-882, *Domain Names - Concepts and Facilities*, by Paul Mockapetris, dated November 1983. This RFC introduces domain style names, their use for Internet mail and host address support, and the protocols and servers used to implement domain name facilities.

RFC-883, *Domain Names - Implementation and Specification*, by Paul Mockapetris, dated November 1985. This RFC discusses the implementation of domain name servers and resolvers, specifies the format of transactions, and discusses the use of domain names in the context of existing mail systems and other network software.

RFC-921, *Domain Name System Implementation Schedule - Revised*, by Jon Postel, dated October 1984. This memo is a policy statement on the implementation of the Domain Style Naming System on the Internet.

RFC-973, *Domain System Changes and Observations*, by Paul Mockapetris, dated January 1986. This RFC documents updates to Domain Name System specifications RFC-882 and RFC-883, suggests some operational guidelines, and discusses some experiences and problem areas in the present system.

RFC-974, *Mail Routing and the Domain System*, by Craig Partridge, dated January 1986. This RFC describes how mail systems on the Internet are expected to route messages based on information from the domain system described in RFCs 882, 883, and 973.

RFC-982, *Guidelines for the Specification of the Structure of the Domain Specific Part (DSP) of the ISO Standard NSAP Address*, an ANSI Working Document X3S3.#/85-258, dated April 1986. This RFC specifies a recommended syntax and interpretation for the Domain Specific Part of an NSAP address.

RFC-854, *TELNET Protocol Specification*, by J. Postel and J. Reynolds, dated May 1983.

RFC-855, *TELNET Option Specifications*, by J. Postel and J. Reynolds, dated May 1983.

RFC-856, *TELNET Binary Transmission*, by J. Postel and J. Reynolds, dated May 1983.

RFC-857, *TELNET Echo Option*, by J. Postel and J. Reynolds, dated May 1983.

RFC-858, *TELNET Suppress Go Ahead Option*, by J. Postel and J. Reynolds, dated May 1983.

RFC-859, *TELNET Status Option*, by J. Postel and J. Reynolds, dated May 1983.

RFC-860, *TELNET Timing Mark Option*, by J. Postel and J. Reynolds, dated May 1983.

RFC-861, *TELNET Extended Options - List Option*, by J. Postel and J. Reynolds, dated May 1983.

Index

- B -

- C -

- D -

- E -

- Z -